Guiding Principles

This book's notes on *The Ancient Magus' Bride* are based on the following guiding principles.

Respect for the originality of the work:

The Ancient Magus' Bride draws on Celtic and European myth and folklore, taking inspiration from history and traditional representations of magic. At the same time, *Magus* is an original fantasy that remixes these elements in its own unique ways. This book differentiates between these approaches with notes such as "In this story/work" and "In mythology."

The guidebook authors (Tokita and Nishigami) feel an original story is free to do whatever most enriches it and makes it most interesting for its audience.

Critique as a romance manga:

The Ancient Magus' Bride is the story of a human girl named Chise and an inhuman mage named Elias Ainsworth. As suggested by the title and [Japanese] slogans such as "a fantasy of otherworldly matrimony" and "inhuman meets girl," a romance between Chise and Elias is a main element of the series. Therefore, one of the angles we're viewing the work from is as a fantasy romance manga of the 2010s.

A Note Before We Begin!

Reading The Ancient Magus' Bride

This *Supplement* aspires to enhance your enjoyment of Kore Yamazaki's original manga *The Ancient Magus' Bride* by providing detailed chapter-by-chapter notes delving into the array of other sources the series draws upon, including mythology, magic, and other such things, to help readers better understand the story.

This was undertaken in the spirit of established approaches to literary criticism that are used both here and elsewhere. Overseas, many books of this sort are published as *The Annotated [Title, Author]*.

This handy book does contain spoilers, so please make sure you're caught up on the manga before reading any further! The manga truly is a masterpiece! We hope this book can increase your enjoyment and understanding of *The Ancient Magus' Bride*.

Supplement II annotates chapters 15-29 (roughly three volumes' worth), going page by page. *Supplement I* covered the manga up to chapter 14, so this picks up where it left off.

Topics that call for more than a brief note are addressed in discussion boxes or sidebars. Within the actual notes, what requires annotation varies depending on the story content, so topics that call for minimal explanation, story-wise, are separated out for further discussion.

A glimpse of life in the United Kingdom:

Elias and Chise live in a large house in the countryside west of London, on the shores of England. The depiction of rural British life is one of many appealing aspects of the story, so this book includes some supplementary explanations of life in the United Kingdom for readers who live in Japan. We hope that it helps you discover the appeal of the U.K. as the plot unfolds for Chise.

Languages:

Because *The Ancient Magus' Bride* is set primarily in the Celtic cultural region surrounding the United Kingdom, it features a great deal of English, as well as drawing on the Gaelic languages native to the Celtic peoples, and Latin, which is often used for alchemical and mythological terms.

The Gaelic languages belonged to the ancient Celts, in particular those who lived on and around the island of Britain. These were the native languages in the regions that are now Ireland, Scotland, and the Isle of Man, but are no longer widely spoken; however, through education and research, efforts at reviving or preserving them and protecting the traditional Celtic cultures are ongoing.

We discuss issues with the term "Celt" in detail in Discussion 1 (p8-11).

The Ancient Magus' Bride

✦ Supplement II ✦

Contents

Table of

Character Introductions

RUTH

Chise's familiar. He willingly bound himself to Chise, sharing everything with her.

CHISE HATORI

Our protagonist. At 15, Chise sold herself at auction, where she was purchased by Elias. She's human, but a rare type known as a "sleigh beggy."

SILKY

A brownie, or domestic spirit, who lives in Elias' house. She communicates with gestures rather than speaking. Always clad in white, she is called either Silky or Silver Lady.

ELIAS AINSWORTH

The mage who purchased Chise at the auction in order to make her his student. He also claimed he plans to make her his bride.

ALICE

An apprentice alchemist, and Renfred's student and bodyguard. Things that happened in her past made her fiercely loyal to him.

MIKHAIL RENFRED

A one-armed alchemist, well known for his hatred of mages. Alice is his student. He and Elias have a history.

LEANNÁN SIDHE

A type of faerie that haunts young men, awakening their poetic talents in return for their lives. This one fell in love with Joel and has stayed by his side.

JOEL GARLAND

An elderly widower who lives alone in a house surrounded by roses, in a town near Elias' home.

LINDEL

One of the few true mages, and Elias' friend. As the caretaker of the dragons' aerie, he hides it from mortal eyes. He thinks of Chise as a granddaughter and looks out for her.

Part 1

within this volume, unless otherwise specified, the term "Celt" is used in the cultural or literary sense, rather than archeological or anthropological senses.

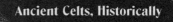

Ancient Celts, Historically

Let us talk about the Celts in history.

Historically, archeologically, and anthropologically, the Celtic people were one of the megalithic cultures of ancient Europe, carrying on the traditions of Hallstatt and La Tène.

Between the 7th and 8th centuries, a warrior tribe wielding iron weapons appeared in Europe. Their arrival had a profound cultural impact on the bulk of Europe (other than the Mediterranean and Scandinavia).

This tribe were a dolichocephalic northern people who spread far through the central and eastern areas north of the Alps, but they were not a monolithic people, nor did they have anything approaching a unified culture. There was no unifying government, only bands of warriors led by local chiefs. The Celtic world was thus a traditional warrior culture speaking the Celtic language, and this spread to the various people they conquered, who gradually came to share their culture and language.

Historically speaking, the first document to name the Celts was by the Greek historian Hecataeus (550-475 BC), referring to a people dwelling to the north of Greece, using the word "Keltoi." This was

DISCUSSION 1: Regarding the Word "Celt"

The Ancient Magus' Bride is set primarily in England, and is heavily influenced by Celtic faerie stories. However, it should be noted that in recent years, use of the word "Celt" as a blanket term has been subject to critical examination.

Many people hearing the word "Celt" immediately think of Ireland. Ireland is famous for Celtic culture, which is a major part of the country's cultural identity, but the word encompasses far more than that.

"Celt" refers to both people who have kept the ancient ways of the European mainland and people who have kept ancient and medieval ways on the islands of Britain and Ireland. To distinguish the two, the former can be referred to as Continental Celts and the latter as Insular Celts, but as the two groups are not genetically linked and there's minimal cultural overlap, these terms are of limited usefulness, if not misleading. Discussion and debate regarding better terminology are ongoing.

While this is going on, the "Insular Celts" (those of Ireland, Wales, etc.) have been at work preserving or reviving the ancient ways, creating a modern Celtic Revival.

In short, the word "Celt" covers a number of groups and concepts. The Celtic tales that influence *The Ancient Magus' Bride* come from the Insular Celts, so

In more recent years, analysis has suggested that despite a few cultural similarities between the Continental and Insular Celts, they were really quite different. It's clear that their mythologies have extremely minimal overlap, and the ruins found in their respective regions reveal very different designs. Even at the genetic level, Continental and Insular Celts are different peoples. It's now believed the two groups are similar but fundamentally distinct, in much the same way as China and Japan have some cultural overlap but are fundamentally independent of each other.

Some Celt-Related Definitions

Celtic People: Term for a people in the megalithic culture of ancient Europe before the advent of Christianity. They are referred to frequently in documents from the Greek and Roman ages, famously in Caesar's *Gallic Wars*, but rather than being a specific people, they were a variety of tribes that spoke Celtic-derived Indo-European languages, inhabited Western and Central Europe, and frequently moved around.

They lived during Europe's Iron Age, and were closely linked to the cultures of Hallstatt and La Tène (the remains of which were discovered in the late 19th century), but that doesn't indicate that they were the same group. There was no central government, and many tribes derived from a Greek word meaning "hidden," so they were being called "the hidden people." These first documents may be Greek because the Celts forbade the use of the written word to pass on their knowledge; Celtic history, thoughts, laws, and rules were all passed by word of mouth. In recent years other explanations have also been put forward, but it is clear they had no written language prior to the Roman age.

The key thing to note here is that those called "Celts" did not use the term to refer to themselves.

Later, as the Roman age began and the non-Roman parts of Europe (the Iberian Peninsula, France, German, Britain, etc.) began to fall, the people in what are now France and Germany either followed the Greeks' lead in using the term "Celts" or referred to that group as the Gauls. A representative source is the *Gallic Wars* written by Julius Caesar in the 1st century BC.

However, these were but scattered tribes, and there was no single body ruling all of the Celts. Even where the Roman Empire was concerned, some tribes fought against Rome while others allied themselves with the Romans.

As mentioned earlier, until the 20th century, Celts and Celtic tribes native to Europe and their cultures were referred to as Continental Celts, and Celtic culture around the British Isles as Insular Celts. In that light, the old culture seen in places like Ireland and Wales can be viewed as Insular Celtic culture. There is a modern Celtic literary movement that carries on or resurrects this ancient Celtic culture.

languages into P-Celtic (Irish, Scots Gaelic, and Manx) and Q-Celtic (Welsh, Cornish, and Breton).

Celtic Myths: The designation for mythology primarily originating from Ireland (known previously as Hibernia and Éire), Scotland (Alba), Wales (Cymru), Britannia, Cornwall, and Brittany. These can be further divided into Irish, Welsh, Cornish and Breton mythology.

Irish mythology is divided into three ages and is the story of six peoples, as described in *The Book of Invasions* (including the story of the Tuatha Dé Danann); the Ulster Cycle, which tells the stories of Cúchulainn and Medb; and the Fenian cycle, stories of the Fianna that feature Fionn mac Cumhaill, Diarmuid, and Sadhbh.

Welsh mythology is primarily represented by the four histories included in the *Mabinogion* (including the *Four Branches of the Mabinogi*). This contains three romances set in the court of King Arthur, some of the earliest Arthurian legends. These spread through Europe, were rewritten as tales of chivalry, and became the stories we know today.

Cornish and Breton mythology also have Arthurian myths, as well as the story of the city of Ys, swallowed by the sea. The book *Celt no Suimyaku* by Kiyoshi Hara starts with a detailed description of the Celtic faith as it survives in Brittany and is good further reading if the topic interests you. The many points of syncretism from later dominant religions like

were conquered by Romans, or either swallowed by the migration of Germanic tribes or absorbed into them, vanishing entirely. What remained of their culture was initially categorized into Continental or Insular groups, but the genetic evidence doesn't support this, and many now believe this to be an inaccurate distinction.

Celtic Language: One branch of Indo-European languages. Similar to Germanic, but with obvious-enough differences that it is considered distinct. According to Pierre-Yves Lambert, they were divided into the Continental languages Golassecca (Lepontic) and Celtiberian and the Insular languages Gallo-Brittonic and Gaelic (Goidelic). Continental languages were spoken before the time of Christ, but as speakers were absorbed into the Roman Empire, the languages are believed to have been lost.

Gallo-Brittonic is related to the Breton language that is still spoken in parts of England and the Brittany region of France. It is unrelated to English, which is a Germanic language.

Even Gaelic, the most well-known of the Celtic languages, is divided into Irish (spoken in Ireland), Manx (on the Isle of Man), and Scots Gaelic (spoken in Scotland). In ancient times they had no writing system and borrowed letters from Latin, while Insular Celtic developed the Ogham alphabet (some say by simplifying the Latin one).

There is an additional theory, based on pronunciation, which divides the in the tides of Romanticism and heightened by the mystic elements common to Irish folktales. This, in turn, occasionally distorted the historical facts and led to academic confusion, but at the same time the movement spread Celtic fairytales far and wide, inspiring the imaginations of fantasy writers the world over.

Christianity and the Greco-Roman myths are fascinating.

Celtic Fairytales: The designation for myths related to faeries that remain in Ireland and the British Isles. Despite being from Christian nations, the stories demonstrate an awareness of mysterious magical beings nearby and emphasize living in harmony with them. These are not just folktales. We also have epic poems like Edmund Spenser's *The Faerie Queene* and plays like William Shakespeare's *A Midsummer Night's Dream*, leading to 20th-century Celtic literature like William Butler Yeats' *The Celtic Twilight* and onwards into modern fantasy.

Technically the origins of these fairytales go back to myths about the Tuatha Dé Danann, but they're influenced by all of Celtic mythology and have become stories distinct from these origins.

Celtic Revival: In modern times, the Celts have been reevaluated as the foundational culture of Europe. A number of Celtic ruins were discovered in the 19th century in Hallstatt and La Tène, shattering the idea that the Celts could be dismissed as barbarians.

Particularly in Ireland, Celtic culture was studied and reevaluated as part of their national identity, and attempts were made to revive the Irish language, sparking the Irish Literary Revival. This movement is a large part of why so many people think of Irish mythology when they hear the word "Celt." This movement was caught

CHAPTER **15** We live and learn.

SUMMARY

A selkie arrives on dragonback, bearing a message from Elias' master, the mage Lindel. In order to make her wand, Chise set off on a journey without Elias, heading to the dragons' aerie in Iceland. She cuts a branch from a tree herself, and begins carving the wand.

In Chise's absence, Elias finds his house perplexingly chilly. An avian familiar arrives from the college—an alchemist society—bearing a message concerning Chise's future.

While Lindel works on her wand, Lindel learns that Elias has told her little to nothing about mages, so as a bedtime story, he tells her how he first met Elias. It began a long time ago, when Lindel was following the reindeer across the snow and encountered the nameless shadow he would come to call "Elias."

General Remarks

Chapter 15 begins the wand-making arc.

Led by Lindel's messenger, a selkie, Chise rides a dragon to Iceland on her own to make her wand. It's the first time since *Magus* began that she and Elias are separated for any length of time, and it gives them each a chance to consider what the other means to them. In particular, Chise is given a glimpse into Elias' past, which adds a new layer to her relationship with him.

Chapter Title

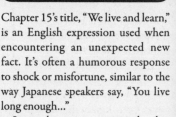

Chapter 15's title, "We live and learn," is an English expression used when encountering an unexpected new fact. It's often a humorous response to shock or misfortune, similar to the way Japanese speakers say, "You live long enough..."

It can also serve as a reminder that we never stop learning, no matter how long we live. In that sense, it's similar to the Japanese saying that literally means "Eighty but still learning," which is often used to encourage lazy young people to work or study, as if to say, "Stop slackin' and get crackin'!"

In this chapter, the phrase means that however long someone lives, they will still encounter new things, just as Chise learns how to make a wand and learns about the origins of mages from Lindel, and just as Elias, who has lived a very long time, learns what loneliness feels like in Chise's absence.

2 "We're nearly there."

When flying from England to Iceland, most of the distance is over the ocean after one leaves the British Isles behind, so there's no spot to rest until you reach Iceland itself. The presentation makes it look like they flew straight from Elias' house to Iceland, but in fact they rested in Scotland and the Faroe Islands. We can assume the full journey took eight to ten hours.

The distance from England to Iceland is roughly 1800 kilometers, and would take about three hours by plane.

3 Title Page

English winter landscape, not seen much in the main narrative.

Chise and Elias face each other from either end of a bridge, each holding a package. Presumably these are Christmas presents, so this is an image of something that didn't occur in the main storyline. Regardless, it symbolizes some key things contained in this small arc of the story.

1 Chise on the Dragon

In a dramatic leap from the end of chapter 14, we see Chise riding a gaoth arach, flying over an Icelandic gorge (gjá). There are many such gjá in the rift valley found in the Þingvellir national park, so it's possible that they're flying over it.

There's much debate over whether a dragon of this size could fly with its wings alone, but the wings are merely symbolic. Dragons are, by their nature, intrinsically tied to the laws that govern the world; it seems appropriate to assume that this allows them to perform the uncommon art of flying. However, gaoth arach are able to fly by passing through the gaps between two winds, so they don't need any magic to fly.

We can assume Ruth is manifested behind Chise (rather than hiding in her shadow), because she is secured only by a blanket and a leather strap and he wouldn't want to risk her falling off.

until volume 7. His speech bubbles have musical notes because selkies are a species that sing. Even with real-world seals, the males will sing to females when courting.

7 "I believe I've said they make opening the gate easier."

Magic in this series involves interacting with the laws of the world and using them to alter reality. Connecting to these laws is often described as "opening the gate."

8 "Yes. They help clarify what we want and specify our goals with precision."

Alchemically speaking, objects such as magic wands are support tools that provide a focal point or focus. (The plural is "foci.")

9 "I didn't say that. I'll go."

She doesn't say that she *wants* to go. She just agrees to follow his instructions.

Chise survived on her own for some time, so being alone isn't an issue, but she does feel a little nervous about not having

4 "Reindeer?"

Mammalia Artiodactyla Cervidae Rangifer are a large type of deer that live all around the North Pole, in Iceland, Scandinavia, Siberia, and Canada. The Japanese name, "tonakai," comes from the Ainu "townakai." Around Japan, they are found in Kamchatka and Siberia. The kanji name is 馴鹿 (junroku, running deer). Reindeer can be as tall as 150 and weight as much as 300 kg.

5 "He's acting like Elias!"

Lindel's line, "Don't I look dashing now?" echoes Elias' line in volume 1, where he first takes human form and says, "How do I look? Handsome? Dashing?" Chise notices their use of the same word.

6 Lady Robin

One nickname the fae use for Chise, a sleigh beggy.

The speaker here is Lindel's familiar, a selkie from Irish folklore. His name is Merituuli, although that isn't mentioned

seal kingdom. There he found the seal he'd injured, and when he put his hand on the wound it was healed. The seals promised that if he stopped hunting them, they'd ensure he lived a life of comfort. The fisherman promised and was given a bag of pearls, living happily ever after.

11 "Dragon hatchlings grow in all sorts of ways!"

In this series, magic power makes wishes come true, and here we see fantasy creatures making use of that power. The magic that can enable such large bodies to fly can also control their growth.

In the same panel we can see Ruth sniffing him in greeting, as they have only just met.

Elias with her. To some that might seem like a minor distinction, but it's significant to Chise.

10 Selkies

Selkies are spirits found in legends in Scotland, Ireland, and the Faroe Islands. "Selkie" is derived from the Gaelic word for "seal." Most of the time they dwell in the ocean, in the form of seals, but occasionally they come up on land, where they shed their seal skins and become beautiful men and women, seducing local young people. There are many stories in which human men who discover selkie's nature hide their skins and take them as brides.

There's also a folktale in Scotland about a Celtic fisherman being taken to the kingdom of the seals at the bottom of the sea. In the story, the fisherman tried to catch a seal, stabbing it in the process, but it escaped. A few days later, a man appeared and asked for a favor, and when the fisherman went with him, they both become seals and soon arrived at the underwater

15   14   13   12

mice and rats and have been common pets since ancient Egypt. While they were kept to protect scrolls and grains from rodents, there's also a long history of them being doted on. They were worshipped in ancient Egypt as the goddess Bastet, but there were also instances of people having their pet cats mummified with them.

Even in Japan, pet cats were kept for pest control, but it often happened that a cat borrowed from another home for that purpose would get very quiet. Since cats see a home as their territory and are sensitive to changes in their environment, they can become guarded and cautious when transplanted out of their territory.

15 "This is a nursery and a haven for dragons, built in one of the many deep rifts—or 'gjá'—in Iceland."

"Gjá" means "rift" and is used to describe the gorges found in Iceland's rift valleys. They're tremendously impressive and are the one place that shows the split between the North American and Eurasian tectonic plates.

12 Elias in the easy chair

Feeling left out, but not knowing how to express that emotion—just feeling the distance between them.

13 "Elias...?"

Elias doesn't have the vocabulary to express his feelings, and his bone face betrays no emotions either, but that doesn't mean he doesn't feel them. From the angle he holds his head or from how talkative he is, Chise can sense these things, so she's aware he's not acting like himself.

14 "I hear that in the east, they sometimes describe someone as being 'meek as a borrowed cat.'"

A Japanese expression used when someone is behaving in a much more subdued manner than usual.

Since cats protect sacred texts from mice, they were brought to Japan along with Buddhism, and became quite common. Small, nocturnal, and carnivorous, cats are an effective countermeasure against

20   19   18 17   16

18 "We'll need to add some other elements—some things with history."

As a focal point for magic, a wand needs multiple conceptual layers. The "history" is the conceptual power of the wood.

What's more, combining woods of different strengths is a good way to make the final wand more durable.

19 "It's best to personally cut the wood for one's own wand!"

Mages have a deep connection to nature. They generally make their own magical items, pouring magic into the final product, which results in something entirely on their wavelength. By making it with their own hands, it becomes a part of them.

What he's given Chise is a tool similar to a billhook.

20 "Humans and dragons are so different from each other…"

Chise's experience with Nevin was deeply emotional, so finding him transformed into a giant tree rattles her.

In 930 AD, Iceland's rift valley—a sort of Icelandic shrine—was also the site of the first meeting of the Althing, the Icelandic national parliament.

16 "That's Nevin's tree."

In volume 1, the dragon Nevin's life ran its course and he returned to the earth. Chise witnessed his death and flew through the sky in a vision they shared at the moment of his passing.

17 "Linden wood isn't suited for construction, but it's good for art."

The Japanese word "bodaiju" is most commonly used for the Chinese-exported *Tiliamiqueliana*, or for the *Ficus religiose*, the tree the Buddha sat under when he attained enlightenment. In Europe, it generally refers to the related species *Tilia × europaea*, the common linden. The bark is used for fiber, and the wood itself is soft and malleable, so it's often used for instruments and carving. That's what Lindel means by "good for art."

This may also be why a mage of song chose to take his name from the tree.

27 **26** **25** **24** **23** **22** **21**

24 **"It's terribly quiet today."**

Humans' very existence generates noise. Their absence makes everything feel quiet.

If Chise were there, he'd be able to feel her presence, and that would be a form of warmth.

25 **"Perhaps I should lay a fire in the hearth."**

A common method of heating European homes. Hearths are made of stone, brick, and metal—inflammable materials—so that kindling can be safely set afire. The smoke goes up the chimney.

Elias feels Chise's absence like the cold of winter, which brings on these idle thoughts.

26 **"A bird?"**

Some mages and alchemists use small animals to deliver messages. Since they can fly, birds make excellent messengers. In this case, it's an artificial creation made from a dead bird.

21 **"Getting a little too friendly with a rock won't kill her!"**

Applying the rough-and-tumble sensibilities of the locals to city kids never ends well.

Ruth argues with Merituuli like a protective older brother, much like Ulysse's relationship with Isabel.

22 **"I'm going to give it another shot."**

The way Chise speaks here shows that she's steadily becoming more independent.

23 **"Thank you, Silver Lady."**

Another name for Silky.

The steam rising from the cup suggests warm tea, but since there's no sign of a spoon, milk, or tea, perhaps this is broth. On cold days, some like to add a shot of whisky to warm broth.

when simmered, and is considered quite tasty. Here it's been stewed with salt, pepper, and a few herbs.

The potatoes have also been boiled until soft and then mashed. Potatoes come from high ground in South America, so they can be raised even in cold regions. They also last a long time and require far less work to be made edible than grains do.

In Japan, reindeer are kept as livestock in Hokkaido, and their meat is shipped around the country in winter.

29 "So that's why your church doggie made such a fuss earlier!"

Ruth is often called a Black Dog, but his kind are also called church grims. Merituuli is clearly aware of that.

30 "He hasn't explained a single thing to you, has he?!"

Becoming a mage's apprentice means multiple things. For that matter, what *is* a mage? How does one become a mage? Surely someone needs to explain these things!

Perhaps Elias sounds questioning because he can tell the bird is a magical construct.

27 "A pleasure to meet you. I am Adolf Stroud, from the college's administration department."

The college is both an alchemy research society and an educational facility.

If you read the *Official Guide Book Merkmal*, you'll be able to read the long-lost rejected draft for chapter 1 of *Magus* and learn that a story in which Chise learns magic at this college has been around from the beginning.

As a fan of the *Circle of Magic* series by Debra Doyle and James D. Macdonald, this is very in character for Kore Yamazaki.

The administration department handles the college's general operations as well as admissions.

28 "It's reindeer stew and mashed potatoes."

Reindeer are a valuable source of protein in the Artic region. The meat grows soft

35 **34** **33** **32** **31**

33 Chise's monologue

Chise finally discusses her past and how her family abandoned her. This is an important confession.

The rejection by her mother, the loss of her father and brother, and rejection from everyone else around her...

To show the isolation and powerlessness Chise felt, Lindel is not depicted on this page.

34 "No one but Elias."

The white background in this panel may symbolize the rejection Chise felt from the world.

Only Elias stands with her.

He may have purchased her, but she was so alone that even that act was enough to satisfy her need for validation and to save her.

35 "That's why..."

Survivors of violence and abuse often focus only on self-preservation, keeping themselves from recognizing the flaws of

31 "Ignorance truly is bliss. Anyone would keep their innocence if they could."

All creatures are naturally drawn to easier (more cost-efficient) ways of going through life. This is but one such way.

32 "A person who ceases to think for herself is no longer truly a person."

It may be a bit of a stretch to say that "thought" is what separates humans and animals, but is seen as one difference between humans and livestock.

If someone allows anxiety about their own existence to make them stop thinking and become entirely dependent on someone else, it's the equivalent of putting their life in somebody else's hands, which could be interpreted as a form of domestication.

This is not the path a mage with power should follow, nor a terribly human way to live.

In this tale, magic is often a miracle brought about by wishing, and frequently utilized without full understanding of how it functions. But to wish for something requires knowledge and understanding, and using magic without those things lessens the effectiveness. However, this may not hold true when praying to a divine spirit.

39 "No one knows why we live so long or are so robust."

It's possible mages were a different species entirely—an entirely separate race. Maybe later volumes will offer some hints or answers to Chise's questions.

40 "Several of our kind have lost themselves in that search."

Perhaps mages are not human, or perhaps they are a race of humans. But either way, they're still people, so they naturally wonder what the reason for their existence is and struggle to find the answers they yearn for.

If they became "lost," that implies that they have served their purpose. They were only able to do so because their purpose was fulfilled.

their temporary guardians while trying to mold themselves into what those guardians demand of them. It can be seen as a form of Stockholm Syndrome, but it is also a type of habitual powerlessness often seen with chronic abuse.

36 "And for some reason, some of us lived far, far longer than a human's normal lifespan."

Until modern times, the average human lifespan was less than fifty years. In contrast, mages living for centuries shows just how unusual they are.

37 "Back then, the hills and fields were alive with fae who would gladly lend us their power."

Magic in *The Ancient Magus' Bride* involves borrowing power from faeries, spirits, and gods to change reality, so this was an age overflowing with magic.

38 "We gained knowledge at the knees of those who were older and wiser than us."

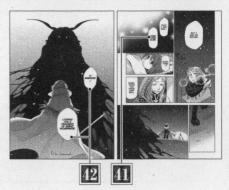

hymn. The national language is Icelandic. The capital is Reykjavik.

The island was once uninhabited, but between 870-930 AD it began to be settled by Vikings, and in 930 a legislative and judicial assembly called the Althing was established. This was a direct democratic body.

In the centuries that followed, it fell under the control of Norway and Denmark, but became independent in 1918, entering an alliance with Denmark. In 1940, Denmark was occupied by Nazi Germany, and Iceland by the British. In 1944, the Republic of Iceland was established. Currently, they are not part of the EU, but are in the EEA (European Economic Area) and part of the Schengen Agreement. They work closely with Northern Europe, Greenland, the Faroe Islands, and Northwestern Europe.

Viking culture has survived comparatively intact, and the Norse mythological epic poem "Edda" was said to have been recorded in Iceland.

Reference: Republic of Iceland Japanese Embassy, Ministry for Foreign Affairs.

That said, not all mages are aware of this. They may simply have a hunch that this is possible.

41 "Something else."

Elias is not yet himself.
He is more monster than mage.

42 "Like a fragment of night incarnate."

A sketch of horror.
In ancient times, the night was a terrifying thing.

The Republic of Iceland

A republic on the island of Iceland in the North Atlantic, which includes Iceland itself and the smaller islands surrounding it.

The total area is 103,000 square kilometers, a little larger than Hokkaido. The population is 340,055 (as of 2019), and 80% are part of the state religion, a Lutheran body, or otherwise Christian. The national anthem is reminiscent of a

SUMMARY

At Lindel's invitation, Chise has left Elias' home and gone to Iceland to make a magic wand. Alone in England, Elias struggles to find the words for his emotions, but finds nothing more suitable than "cold."

Meanwhile, in Iceland, Chise listens to Lindel's story of how he met Elias—a "fragment of night incarnate" that appeared out of nowhere. Lindel found himself unable to abandon the thing that would eventually become Elias, and together, they visited his master, Rahab. All Rahab is able to tell them is that Elias is something like a fae or spirit. She gives Elias his name and orders Lindel to take Elias as his apprentice. Lindel refuses to accept that arrangement, but the two travel together as friends.

At one point, a year later, Lindel approaches a village in search of food only to have a child spy Elias hiding in his shadow and mistake him for a devil. Lindel is driven out of town and injured, and to protect him, Elias unleashes his own power. That night, Elias confesses that he may have eaten humans in the past.

General Remarks

The second chapter of the wand-making arc delves deeper into Elias' past. It offers an important expansion of the story's background, covering Elias and Lindel's first meeting, the origins of Elias' name, and his relationship with Lindel.

Chise is already aware of how other faeries scorn Elias, and now this story of long-ago events in a village make her aware that he may be a man-eating monster.

This is the start of volume 4.

Chapter Title

Once bitten, twice shy" is an expression used in all English-speaking territories. People naturally become cautious after being hurt, as in the situation where someone who's been bitten by a dog may become afraid of dogs in general.

This phrase was used as the title of a 1975 song by the English singer Ian Hunter, as well as in Wham!'s "Last Christmas." It's also been used as a title in a wide array of genres. Sometimes only the first half ("Once Bitten") is used, although the connotations don't really change. Another similar expression is "A burnt child dreads the fire."

A similar Japanese expression is one that roughly translates as "learn from hot soup and blow on cold."

Elias met Lindel and was given a name, but while the two were spending time together, Elias' memories of his dark man-eating past surfaced. Those memories are one reason why he's so cautious in his dealings with humans.

2 Title Page

Chise in a panel of her own, looking over at a panel depicting Elias in the past—a bold layout illustrating the core structure of the wand-making arc.

Elias already appears as if he might be wearing clothing, but it's not certain that he's actually wearing anything at all.

3 Reindeer Meat

While Lindel traveled across the snow, his cooking largely consisted of stewed reindeer or dried meats, mushrooms, and berries.

The dishes used are made of wood and don't conduct much heat, so he can hold a bowl of hot stew like this without burning himself. Wooden dishes are cheaper and easiest to obtain than porcelain or metal, are sturdy, and are easy for him to make or adjust himself. What's more, in such frigid temperatures, porcelain or metal dishes might well get cold enough to give him frostbite.

By the way, if you look closely at the

1 "All young folk with magical or alchemical gifts…"

The word "college" usually refers to higher-learning institutes, and the Japanese system treats them as distinct from universities (which have graduate schools attached). But the college in this series is also a mutual-aid collective.

Humans occupying certain fields often tend to form societies to provide leadership and share ideas. A school seeking to organize mages and alchemist is no exception, but since Elias is not human, it has no power over him.

Where mages interact directly with the natural laws, alchemists in this series use logic and formulas to alter the world; to them, societies that organize information and educate apprentices are a vital resource, but expecting the same response from a mage is barking up the wrong tree. Yet here they are attempting to use this as an excuse to bring Chise under the watchful eye of the college.

Prussia became Polish territory until the Third Reich demanded Poland return the land, and set off the Second World War.

5 England

A country on the southern end of the island of Great Britain, one of the four countries that make up the United Kingdom today. Many people use "England" and "United Kingdom" interchangeably, but this is incorrect.

Given that Russia, Prussia, France, and England are mentioned here, we can assume these events occurred before the Russian Revolution, in a time when Prussia was leading Germany. In 1707, England and Scotland merged into the Kingdom of Great Britain, so this is likely before that.

6 Elias Fixating on Lindel's Throat

Dogs and other carnivores regularly secure food by going for their prey's throats. Even as he says, "I am tired," Elias may still find Lindel appetizing.

dining scene after this, you'll see that the shape of Elias' head doesn't lend itself to eating. With no cheeks, he can't use his teeth to chew. It seems likely he has to swallow everything whole.

4 Prussia

A land along the Baltic from eastern Germany to western Poland. The name comes from the Prussians, who lived there for a very long time. In the 13th century, with the Kingdoms of Poland and Lithuania against them, they entered the protection of the Teutonic Order and became known as the State of the Teutonic Order. For some time, Germany and Poland traded rights to the territory, occasionally reestablishing it as the Duchy of Prussia or Royal Prussia, but in the 19th century it became the Kingdom of Prussia and the core of the North German Confederation, with King Wilhelm I becoming the German Emperor. In the early 20th century, they were absorbed into the Weimar Republic, which controlled Germany. Split into east and west, part of

While this is depicted with an eye towards humor, Elias' ignorance of the sea shows him as a child who knows little of the world.

9 Rahab

Rahab is the name of a beautiful woman who appears in the Old Testament Book of Joshua. She lived in Jericho and was said to have been a prostitute. When the Hebrews were preparing to attack Jericho, she harbored two spies they sent in. To show their gratitude, the spies told her to hang a red cord over her door. The Hebrew assault was a brutal one, but her family was spared, and they alone survived the massacre. As a red cord is also a symbol of a brothel, this seems to confirm her profession.

In the New Testament Gospel of Matthew, Rahab is mentioned as one of the ancestors of Jesus, and there is much debate over whether she is the same person as the one in Jericho. Dante's *Divine Comedy* depicts her as having been invited into heaven.

7 Spruce

A plant of the Pinaceae family and Picea genus. In Japanese, it usually refers to a variant of the Ezo spruce, but here it refers to a mainstay Northern European coniferous tree, the Norway spruce. A tall evergreen native to Europe, smaller ones resemble firs, and both are often used for Christmas trees. When fully grown, they can reach heights of 50m and have trunks 2m in diameter. There are spruce trees that are more than 9000 years old, and they are considered some of the oldest trees in the world. Their size and impact means they have often been considered trees of great spiritual power that reach to the heavens. Parts of them connect to legends of the world tree that are found all across the globe.

Using red thread is a cantrip from Finland, and using cord is a variation on that.

8 "It's the sea. Have a taste."

Using magic to cross the sea and using magic to search for that which is lost can open paths, a fact that will be important later.

Since they were so often used as gathering spots, there are many place names that include the word. Over 800 towns in Germany have "Linde" as part of their name.

Linden flowers have a pleasant smell, which helps encourage people to gather. Linden honey is a greenish yellow and extremely tasty. Some regions also dry the flowers and use them as herbal tea. They're said to be effective against colds and sore throats, and to help people relax.

Lindel's master Rahab gave him that name in the hopes that he would become more social, but Linden himself chose to live with the reindeer instead.

11 Two Cups

Presumably warm milk.

12 "Red."

Red is the color of blood, and as mammals, humans tend to instinctively react strongly to this color.

This image suggests tragedy to come.

The name Rahab in Hebrew means "noise," "revolt," or "haughty." It also appears in the Psalms and the Book of Isaiah as the name of the sea monster. Though a symbol of chaos, he also helped retrieve the Book of Raziel. This monster (a type of dragon) is said to have been born from the primordial goddess Tiamat in Babylonian legends, and is also said to be one of the guardian deities of Egypt.

10 "A pity, especially as your name's derived from that of the tree of gatherings."

Another name for the linden tree. European lindens can live for over a thousand years, so they are often found in the center of towns, near springs, or near gates, and gatherings were held beneath them. They were a spot for villagers to assemble, for weddings or receptions to be held, or for dancing. On a daily basis people would gather to make small talk. They were also used for trials, hence the German "Gerichtslinde" or "court linden."

14 "Love your enemy."

Words from one of Jesus' sermons, as recorded in the New Testament Gospel of Luke, starting with chapter 6, verse 27.

"But to you who are listening I say: Love your enemies, do good to those who hate you, bless those who curse you, pray for those who mistreat you."

"Neighbors" here refers not to faeries but to fellow humans. The Jews had experienced a lot of conflict with the countries around them and with other tribes. They'd been conquered, taken from their homelands, and forced to live for many years in ways they did not wish. As a result, there was resentment towards other tribes, but Jesus ordered them to free themselves from such emotions.

15 "It's all right. I'll move on."

Reduced to child size, Elias sees that Lindel is upset, and feels as if he should leave.

13 "Russia is waking up."

In the Middle Ages, Norway and Sweden were major countries, boasting powerful armies descended from Vikings. Russia also took on Viking royalty, absorbing nearby leaders and expanding. Prussia and Poland were unable to avoid conflict with Russia. As background for this bit of dialogue, we note that Norway and Sweden's nomadic peoples had once been able to pass unhindered across country lines, but as relationships between the two kingdoms deteriorated, this was no longer the case, and they were forced to settle down. On top of that, Russia was at war with Sweden, with Finland caught in the middle, so there were many reasons why life could not continue as it was.

Additionally, these northern counties were expanding into the snowfields of Siberia in search of valuable furs from otters and silver foxes, invading Lindel's territory.

20   19   18   17

one to tell him what is right, he has a mix of male and female garb, chosen according to his own tastes, including the shoes with the pompoms. The severity of the cold varies in this region, and furs of different thickness are worn at -20 or -40 degrees.

19 "Don't take what you're not going to eat."

Hunters know that the numbers of wild animals are not infinite, and some must be spared. They hunt only what they need and will eat, or else they'll suffer in subsequent years.

At this point Elias still lacks such basic knowledge, and has little concept of the value of life. He isn't yet used to his flesh form.

20 "Stay hidden inside my shadow."

By now Elias already had the ability to hide within shadows. Both Lindel and Rahab understood that Elias' nature was similar to that of shadows.

16 "Elias."

Elias Ainsworth receives his name. Elias is a masculine name derived from the prophet Elijah. Elijah is Hebrew for "The Lord is my God."

Elijah was a prophet in the 9th century BC, when Israel was ruled by King Ahab. He received the word of Yahweh on Mount Horeb and raised up Elisha as his successor. After prophesying that catastrophe would befall Ahab and the Israelis, he vanished. Obeying Yahweh's instructions, Hazeal became king of Syria and Jehu king of Israel.

Elijah was lifted to heavens in a whirlwind, or perhaps carried there on a chariot of fire drawn by horses of fire. This has resulted in legends of Elijah's return.

17 "Here. A charm."

Elias will come to love this sort of neck adornment.

18 Lindel's Clothing

He's wearing the clothing of the Sami people from northern Finland. With no

Rocks were often thrown to protect farms and drive away enemies. Public executions in the Middle East and Europe were often carried out by stoning.

25 Spears of Shadow

Elias's desire to protect Lindel manifests in physical form.

26 "Veil of the forest! Lift thy curtain and allow us to pass!"

A spell offering a prayer to the forest itself, allowing them to pass through the forest's veil and flee into a space out of step with reality. By offering a prayer to those that rule this forest, they can hide beneath the veil. By placing his hands on the snow, he strengthens contact with the land.

27 "The far side of the forest's veil."

Finland tends to view forests as sacred, and forests often cast spells on people. In such cases, the veil has snared them. The veil of the forest is a mixed-up world where the sun rises from the west, rivers flow uphill,

21 "I am a shaman."

Before the word "magic" came into common use, this was a name for practitioners of magic arts. They dealt in curses and charms, and in the lifting of curses. They were also known as witch doctors or medicine men.

22 "That man has a *thing* in his shadow."

Children's eyes can sometimes see things they should not. Their knowledge of the world is still flexible enough that they can sense inhuman things.

23 "Monster! That was a monster posing as a shaman!"

The word translated as "monster" here can also refer to devils, demons, and all manner of creatures that bring harm in folk legend.

24 Throwing Rocks

Rocks may seem primitive, but they're an effective weapon even in modern times.

and be guided by them down to the path to alter reality.

However, this time he directly asked for help from the forest veil. Because no neighbor assisted, he had to use his own power—his own life force—leaving him exhausted.

Neighbors, in this case, could be faeries, spirits, or other types of fae.

30 "The cantrip I once showed him..."

Elias is reproducing the means of finding something lost that Lindel himself once used, searching for a way out.

Since he's relying on memory, the spell itself is quite slapdash, but Elias's own similarity to fae lets him give shape to his magic. Just as it did when Lindel was searching for Rahab, the spruce cantrip begins moving on its own, using the branches as wings.

31 Elias the Nurse

He is boiling water and wiping the wounds with sterilized cloth.

and people must walk with their feet overhead. Should you accidentally step onto a faerie trail, you'll be lost on the inside of the forest veil. Someone caught by the veil will find themselves lost in a place they ought to know, remain dry though it rains, and lose all sense of time. They can perceive people searching for them, but cannot make themselves seen or heard.

To escape the forest veil, you must wear your clothing inside out. Those searching must bind the forest magic by using a red string to tie three spruce branches together.

28 "This is not a place for mortals to tread."

Forcing your way into the realm of gods and fae will earn their wrath, and curses worse than death.

29 "We can use magic without a neighbor's aid, but it's very... very draining..."

Normally, a mage would ask for aid from or pray to a knowledgeable faerie or god

The
Ancient Magus'
Bride
Supplement
II

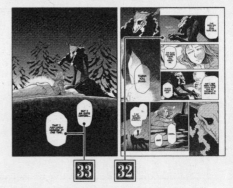

Healing Hands

Among the Sami people (nomadic tribes from Finland who keep reindeer) there are those who are said to heal wounds with just a touch. This ability is called having "healing hands."

According to Sami legend, healing hands are related to frogs. Frogs transform the hands of those with the courage to pick them up, or whose hands they happen to make contact with, into healing hands. The mere touch of such hands on an afflicted body part will quickly ease pain. It's said that when a scab forms, you should place a frog against it and rub it.

In ancient times, many places believed hands had the power to heal; the Japanese word for "treatment," "teate," literally means "to place hands." Sami traditional healing involves massages and hand techniques.

32 **Scrape Scrape**

He is peeling the potatoes with his own claws rather than with a blade, then placing them in the pot. It may look like he is cooking, but that might be putting it generously.

33 **"But I am quite certain that I fed upon humans at one time."**

Elias confesses that he may have eaten humans. Perhaps this is why a part-fae creature like Elias obtained a body of flesh.

This is a fact he admits to a friend he trusts, in his way, but it is also a burden.

SUMMARY

"But I am quite certain that I fed upon humans at one time."

After Lindel reveals the shocking confession Elias once made, Chise mulls it over and accepts it, then resumes work on her wand the next day. When her work is finally finished, Lindel demonstrates magic through singing and Chise is able to watch elves dance.

Chise finds herself wanting to see Elias, and is able to unexpectedly connect with him via a water mirror.

General Remarks

When Chise hears about Elias' man-eating past from Lindel, she seems unsurprised; she saw fae all her life back in Japan, and she never assumed Elias was unlike them.

Under Lindel's guidance, Chise gets so absorbed in making her wand that she loses track of time. While lost in thought, she wishes that she'd done more thinking about her relationship with Elias, and starts to consciously consider her feelings about him. Those emotions build a bridge between her and Elias and allow the two of them to speak through a water mirror.

With Lindel's song as a centerpiece, this is a chapter full of romance that strengthens Elias and Chise's feelings for each other.

Chapter Title

"Lovers ever run before the clock" comes from Shakespeare's *The Merchant of Venice*, Act 2, Scene 6, and it refers to the way time spent with a lover always flies past.

The line is spoken by Gratiano to Salarino, to which Salarino replies, "Oh, ten times faster Venus' pigeons fly to seal love's bonds new-made, than they are wont to keep obliged faith unforfeited."

Doesn't this remind you of the bird of fire we see in chapter 18 of *The Ancient Magus' Bride*?

3 **"Shouldn't you say these things to *him*, not me?"**

Lindel speaks from the heart. This is a subject best discussed by the people involved, not with a third party.

4 **"I probably taste marvelous, but don't eat me, okay?"**

When a person (or something close enough) eats another person (or someone of their own kind) we call it cannibalism.

There are cases of this happening on islands that failed to propagate livestock, or when necessary to survive in times of starvation, but in most cases it remains a taboo.

Ritual cannibalism had a different meaning within some groups. Consuming the body of a member of a collective is known as endocannibalism, which can be a part of the funeral rites, signifying that the participants are carrying on the life of the deceased. One type of this is seen in Japan, with bone-chewing practices. Eating enemies of the collective, or exocannibalism, implies taking on the

1 **Title Page**

A dragon with antlers. Since it lacks wings, we think this is similar to the lindwurm, a type of dragon that appears in Germanic and North European mythology. "Lindwurm" is a word that refers more to a giant snake than a dragon (or "drache" in German), and encompasses the Jörmungandr of Norse legend as well as Fáfnir and Níðhöggr from German epic poetry.

2 **"And it's not uncommon, after time passes, for 'father' to become 'husband' or 'mother' to become 'wife.'"**

That wasn't called for, Lindel. But it's true that when master and apprentice are of opposite genders, they often end up marrying. In particular, mages in the same line of work, who often share similar ways of thinking, often come to see each other as a partner for the ages.

Chise gets what Lindel is implying, but she doesn't yet feel at all like a bride, hence her reaction.

Worshipping beasts that are stronger than humans and prey upon them is a common practice seen the world over. The further north you go, the larger bears get, and the more likely they were to be venerated.

7 "You ought to travel south someday!"

Elias and Lindel met in the north, in what is now Finland or Sweden. Elias eventually took this advice and headed south.

8 "If you go there and try all manner of new flavors…"

To eat is to experience. If Elias wishes to forget the flavor of human flesh, then eating a variety of other delicious foods is the best way to forget the urges he wishes to be free of.

Taking this advice to heart, perhaps Elias should not be staying in England, famed for being home to some of the worst food in the world, but given how much Chise seems to enjoy it, perhaps the Silver Lady's cooking is quite excellent.

strength of the enemies, and is also an expression of revenge.

That aside, Lindel's assertion that he himself must taste marvelous is perhaps a bit excessive.

5 "I do sometimes still feel a craving."

Elias admits he still feels the urge to eat humans sometimes, but this is not so much something he's been consistently conscious of as something he realizes as he answers Lindel's questions. This is a form of training to live with the beast within.

6 "Some people worship bears as gods, for example—even though bears eat humans."

In ancient Europe, bears were venerated as gods of the forest. The name "Art" comes from the word for bear and is said to be the origin of King Arthur's name. Artio, a goddess of the woods, is also worshipped as a forest bear, and there are other goddesses across Europe whose names likewise start with "A."

trial and error where people did things like accidentally eat the potatoes' eyes.

The terrible stench from Elias' stew likely sprang from how badly he handled the ingredients, as well as a failure to skim off the foam.

11 Cut to His Fangs

This panel from chapter 14 shows an expression of animal lust that this chapter connects to Elias' hidden urge to eat humans. But while Chise senses his desire, she's unafraid.

12 "I guess I looked tasty to him?"

She interprets his desire as "tasty." She's not yet thinking in terms of love.

13 "Now I know something that he didn't want to talk about."

Chise is still thinking about how to avoid bothering Elias. She's afraid to upset him by asking about things he'd rather not talk about, and even more afraid that doing so would damage their relationship. Instead she chooses to wait for Elias to volunteer

9 "Any trace of fear vanished with my first mouthful of the stew he'd made me."

Here, Lindel's feelings for Elias are clearly illustrated. A single mouthful of stew banishes his fear of his friend's sins and cannibalism, demonstrating the depth of the bond they'd built.

10 "Which, I might add, was the most disgusting thing I'd ever tasted."

The most common reason that food turns out poorly is mistakes made regarding quantities and steps, followed closely by lack of preparation. It's common for aspiring cooks to ruin dishes by oversalting them. In his haste, Elias didn't cook the stew long enough, so the ingredients didn't cook all the way through and came out hard and unpleasant.

Potatoes arrived in Europe during the Age of Discovery, and people there initially didn't know how to handle them. While potatoes are suited for growing in cold climates, there was a long period of

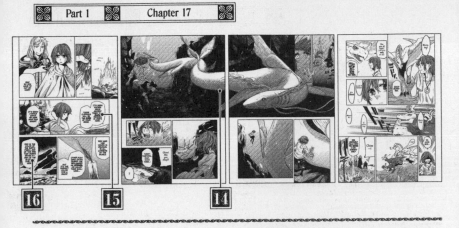

piece of her hair and placed it with his body to protect it. Even after Osiris was resurrected, her long hair covered his head, protecting him.

In the Old Testament Book of Judges, the powerful hero Samson's strength lies in his hair. God commanded him to never cut or shave off his hair, but after Samson shares this information with Delilah, a woman he'd fallen in love with, he was captured by the Philistines when she betrayed his secret to them.

Since aging results in hair turning white or in hair loss, hair is often linked to people's life force. In turn, that is linked to the practice of monks and nuns shaving their heads as a symbol of their rejection of secular things.

16   "Red is the color of the earth itself, and of the fire that burns within it—and of the blood in our own veins."

Humanity knows that the molten rock inside the earth is red. That is the power of the fire the earth spits out.

information. She falls asleep worrying about this, but doesn't reach an answer.

14   The Underwater Dragon

Since the dragons' aerie was created to take care of all dragons, its residents include dragons from other parts of the world. This water dragon originally lived somewhere else, but has been moved here for safekeeping.

European dragons are primarily the fire-breathing type, but like the lindwurm mentioned earlier, there are also a number of dragons viewed as river lords. This water dragon's design resembles river fish, but it's definitely a kind of dragon.

15   "It's been known since ancient times that magic resides in one's hair."

The belief that hair harbors magic is rooted in the belief that hair is linked to the power of the soul. This is one reason why the Japanese keep clippings of hair from the deceased.

When Osiris, husband of the Egyptian goddess Isis, was murdered, she cut off a

21 **20** **19** **18** **17**

rustles in the elongated leaves of the weeping willows is particular distinctive. In Japan, the willow is often associated with refreshing breezes, but in Europe it was often treated as a slightly sinister plant, always growing around the water. The willow belonged to the goddess Hecate (or her maiden aspect, Helike) and is necessary to protect oneself in the afterlife. Orpheus carried willow branches on his trip to Hades.

Willow has been used to lower fevers and as a painkiller since Egyptian/Assyrian times.

19 "Blessed hazel wards off all misfortune."

While the Japanese word describes a small tree that grows across Russia and northern Asia, here it means a shrub of the Betulaceae family, specifically the *Corylus avellane*. The nuts of this tree are called hazelnuts, and are eaten all over the world. Hazel was used in the god Hermes' staff, and is said to be useful in healing and fortune-telling.

That's why we refer to the earth as red, knowing that there's fire underneath.

17 "Dark elderberry is the tree that knocks on the door of a dark goddess."

While the Japanese word used here refers to a shrub of the Adoxaceae family and Sambucus genus, it's specifically meant to indicate *Sambucus racemosa*, the red elderberry. "Elder" comes from the old English "Oeld," or fire. The "dark goddess" here refers to the Celtic goddess Morrígan, wife of the god of death, the Dadga, and ruler of the land of the dead. To knock on her doors means to cast death magic.

18 "Ghostly willow stands twixt the worlds of the living and the dead."

A deciduous tree of the Salicaceae family and Salix genus that grows across the northern hemisphere. Preferring watery lands, it lays down heavy roots, often growing on riverbanks. The way the wind

22

"Nanakamado" is a deciduous tree of the Rosaceae family, Sorbus genus, and the variety widely seen in Europe is called the rowan—an old Norse word for warding off evil. In Norse mythology, the god of thunder, Thor, once survived crossing a flooded river because of a rowan charm made by his wife, Sif. It is believed to protect against watery peril as a result.

In Druidic beliefs, the rowan tree was believed to have protective influence. Because the rowan berries have five points, they are linked to the pentagram. In Neo-Druidism, the rowan is believed to be a portal tree between worlds.

22 "Where elves dance, flowers bloom."

European legends say that circles of flowers appear when faeries dance. These are called fairy rings.

Here the word used specifically refers to elves. Iceland is heavily influenced by Norse mythology, so fae are usually referred to as elves instead. Elves are spirits found in Germanic and Norse mythology.

20 "Eternal yew is a symbol of the ages, beloved of magic and yet capable of banishing it."

Yew is a coniferous evergreen of the Taxaceae family. The Japanese yew is called "ichii" because it was used to make shaku batons for first-ranked ("ichii") nobility; it is also called "araragi." However, the yew here is technically a different plant, the European yew. (Locally, it would be called just "yew.") As a hard softwood that's resistant to water and is long lasting, it was often used for furniture. The berries are edible, but the seeds are poisonous. It is sometimes used to aid with swallowing or as a cough suppressant.

The druids used it as a symbol of eternity and planted it at gathering spots. This has resulted in there often being trees near churches. It was considered a symbol of death and resurrection.

21 "Sturdy rowan has a powerful life force than can subjugate any fae creature."

25 "No more..."

While the elves can dance endlessly, Chise has worn herself out.

Since ritual dance uses magic power, it can take its toll on the children of men. In legends, while the elves dance on and on, humans who join their circle die of exhaustion and keep being twirled around, even in death.

26 Water Mirror

Something appears on the surface of the water. Just as water can be a mirror that shows us our reflection, this art allows water to be used as a mirror that reflects a person far away. Depending on the spellcaster, this might be like talking through a window, or over a gate.

In this case, Lindel's song and the elves' dancing have helped bring Chise's desire to fruition. And since Elias had placed a pot in the yard to collect rainwater and found himself drawn to that place, the final requirement for the magic was fulfilled.

The original words means "white," and words like "albino" and "alps" come from the same root. It's believed that they were originally something like small gods.

23 "Dance with us!"

Dance is something to share, not to simply watch. It's inherently a ritual.

24 "Humanity remembers, Chise. Since before words were born, since before time itself dawned, sound has filled the air...and our bodies remember."

The origins of magic go back to when the world and humanity were one and the same. Humans sensed the sounds that filled the world and danced in time to that beat. To dance is to make one's self one with the earth.

In shamanic religions in particular, dance is an important spell component, the heart of their faith, and the means by which they share their power.

In this work, magic is all about harmonizing with the laws of the world, so dance is very much like magic.

kimono, which hangs close to the ground; it is an expression of modesty, much like the way people giving gifts say, "It's nothing much." "Osuso-wake" is usually used when addressing superiors.

However, Elias and Chise are actually speaking English here, and Japanese idiomatic politeness can be difficult to express in European languages, which is why it comes out in the much more direct "have some."

The Japanese does not use the kanji here, only the hiragana; the nuance conveyed is that Chise is speaking gently, from the heart.

30 "It's only fair that I tell you new things about me."

Chise has made up her mind to tell Elias about her difficult past. Until now, she didn't have the courage to do so, and she didn't want to remember it. She was also afraid that he might not be interested. So many different conflicting emotions! But now that she's heard things about Elias that he might have preferred she not know, she feels strongly that she should in turn tell him the things she'd rather not discuss.

27 "You look...weirdly somber or something."

While Elias' bones have no muscles to show expressions, Chise has learned to read his mood anyway.

28 "The house is cold in your absence."

Elias doesn't share human emotions, and the word "lonely" is not in his vocabulary, so this is how he expresses it. He doesn't understand this emotion yet.

29 "Here, have some!"

Chise would like to leap through the mirror and rejoin him, but instead she scatters flowers on the mirror as a gift to him. Though small, the fact that she was able to send something through the water gate from Iceland to England shows just how strong their connection is.

The Japanese expression used here, "Osuso-wake" (the polite version of "suso-wake") is used when sharing a gift received with others. "Suso" is the hem of a

SUMMARY

With Chise's work done, Lindel finishes her wand.

The wand shows her an illusion, reuniting her with the dragon Nevin. They speak, and in response to her worries, he says, "Then stop fearing that you might trip and tumble up into the sky." In contrast to how Chise often puts herself down, Nevin expresses his gratitude to her, giving her the push she needs to activate her finished wand, transform into a bird of fire, and fly back to Elias.

CHAPTER 18

Better to ask the way than go astray.

General Remarks

The final chapter of the wand-making arc.

Having successfully completed her wand, Chise is shown her a vision of Nevin, and speaking to him allows her to realize what she truly desires, which gives her the courage to fly back home to Elias.

We see proof that absence makes the heart grow fonder.

Chapter Title

"Better to ask the way than go astray" is an English expression suggesting that you should ask for help if you find yourself lost.

If something suspicious or confusing happens, it's best to set pride aside and consult those around you. People tend to overestimate their own ability and be too vain to look for advice or warnings. This English phrase is similar to the Japanese expression, "Asking is a momentary shame; not asking is a lifetime of it."

In this chapter, rather than just fret to herself, Chise confesses her troubles to Nevin, is given the answer she needs, and is able to fly because of it.

from her expressions, and demonstrates the distance between them.

4   Title Page

Chise naked under wings. Birds are Chise's symbol, but don't forget that behind that symbolic imagery lie her bare emotions.

5   "I dozed off."

Chise was sleeping with a dragon hatchling as her pillow. As some dragons in *The Ancient Magus' Bride* are modeled on emus and ostriches, there are varieties that have emu-like thin feathers or fur. As warm-blooded species, they're ideal for sleeping next to.

6   "It's done…?"

Not because the elves helped! More likely she unconsciously used magic to complete the finishing touches.

Note the bird shape on the head. Chise has made a wand that fits the kanji in "Hatori": "wing" and "bird."

1   "All I sought was a convenient human to play at being my apprentice."

And now we see Elias' confession. This is the first time since our tale began that we've seen a glimpse inside Elias' mind.

In his mind's eye, Chise appears even younger.

At first, she was nothing but a way for him to escape the external demands for him to take an apprentice. It was pure coincidence that he chose Chise.

2   "I came across a truly rare specimen."

Chise is a sleigh beggy.

3   "She does not speak much."

Chise, who wasn't skilled at communicating with others and wanted to avoid becoming a burden on Elias, found herself unable to ask the things she wanted to. Unfortunately, Elias was unable to understand why.

This page shows what Elias interprets

10 **9** **8** **7**

9 **"I didn't want to bother him, so I've just been looking stuff up in his books."**

A very Japanese approach, but from the perspective of an instructor, quite risky—it would be better to ask. The master's own perspective on things can be emphasized by answering questions, and the bonds between master and apprentice are strengthened.

Elias' views on this are covered at the start of the chapter.

10 **The Finishing Ritual**

Lindel sings because that's how he performs magic.

He brings magical elements like Chise's hair and the gemstone and incorporates them into the wand. As Lindel says, her hair affects the external appearance.

11 **"Your wand—though it's more a staff at this size—is truly done. Take good care of it."**

A magic wand made with time and effort like this gives it a powerful relationship/

7 **"That's why the objects a mage creates will always be a source of power for them."**

Since mages always have magic around them, things they're in contact with for a lengthy period of time can easily become infused with that magic. That's how magic is transferred to things they create, a process known as enchanting or artificing. If they're making, say, medicine, this results in a stronger or longer-lasting effect. The reason handmade products of any kind have value is because the individual's magic (metaphorically or not) is poured into them.

8 **"So that's what Simon meant..."**

Simon is the priest who monitors Elias, but he has a chronic respiratory condition and relies on Elias' medicine. He's mentioned before that the mage's medicine is very effective.

in the Ninhursag Shrine in the ruins of the Mali Empire. This depicts the goddess Ninhursag seated on a swing. The shrine is 30 centuries old, and this is believed to be the world's oldest depiction of a swing.

Swings are often seen as a symbolic offering to a holy tree in tree worship, and it is believed that before the swing arrived, they used to hang sacrificial girls from the tree.

13 "Little hatchling mage."

English often uses "little" as a term of endearment.

Here the dragon Nevin, who first appeared back in volume 1, speaks to Chise. He has died and returned to the earth, and a linden tree grew out of him. She used a branch of this sacred tree in her wand, and the connection she had to him has great magical significance.

Nevin himself has long since left the world, but he is delighted that a part of himself can be by Chise's side in the form of this wand.

link/bond with the owner. This allows the owner to use it as an extension of themselves, supporting their magic—but that works both ways.

In many fantasy stories, a mage's wand or staff is a part of them, and if that wand is destroyed they're in deep trouble. In *The Ancient Magus' Bride*, magic wands are reliable in a pinch, something that will support them over the long paths that lie ahead.

While English differentiates between "staff" and "wand" based on the size, the Japanese word "tsue" contains no such distinction.

12 A Swing

A swing hanging from a massive tree in the mist is clearly metaphorical on many levels.

In the ancient Mediterranean, swings were a part of tree worship, and a young maiden on a swing hanging from a secret tree was part of a harvest ritual. Once believed to have originated in India, in 1938 a bizarre terracotta statue was unearthed

19   18   17   16 15 14

The world is only beautiful to those who perceive it to be.

Remember, one of the Japanese slogans for *The Ancient Magus' Bride* is, "A story about learning to perceive the world's beauty." Early on, Chise cared little for the world or herself, but she has now begun to see the beauty in it, and she's sharing that with Nevin.

17 "What say you have a go at speaking to yourself?"

It's better to get feelings off your chest, and when you do, it's good to have some sort of protector who will listen to and accept you. In that sense, Nevin is like a grandfather to Chise.

18 "I know I've gotten...well, greedy."

One reason situations of neglect worsen is because victims often give up and try to accept the harmful situation. In feeling that they just need to endure things (and that if they don't, the abuse and discrimination will get worse), they

14 "When you accepted my branch for your wand, a bond formed between us. I called you here."

A critical factor in understanding magic is the power that creates relationships. Wishes, desires, and the threads that bind us allow us to meet again.

The link between Nevin and Chise is strengthened by the handcrafted wand. Then this contact made that wish come true.

15 "This is an interstice."

Reality is not just the physical world we can see. There are other worlds across the boundary lines. This interstice is the boundary between life and death—a world that beings on either side of that boundary can access.

16 "So, this is how your mind perceives it?"

Perceptions of the world depend upon the observer, and especially in this sort of interstice, the interpretations of those beholders can be wildly different.

21   **20**

It's similar to the Japanese word "ki-yuu," which takes two kanji from the Chinese expression "Qǐrényōutiān," or "Qi people lament heaven." It is said that the people of Qi often feared that the sky would fall, and the phrase and word have come to refer to any and all needless fears.

It seems unlikely that an old dragon like Nevin would be aware of this concept. It's more likely that in communicating through the bonds between their hearts, he has received this knowledge from Chise and it was translated into the phrasing above.

21 **"I cannot say if this tendency of yours is something you were born with, or if it is a legacy from your mother."**

Chise has described it as her mother's curse. Curses take effect when the target is made aware of them. Her mother may have started it, but it was Chise who accepted it as a curse.

often give up on ever escaping their circumstances.

Chise has been accepted by Elias, and is hesitantly beginning to reach out once more, but this still scares her, which is why she characterizes it as "greedy."

19 **"I...wish I could have stayed detached."**

The opposite of love is not hate but indifference. This thought reveals how large a place Elias has come to occupy in Chise's mind.

20 **"Then stop fearing that you might trip and tumble up into the sky."**

This is a reversal of the old chestnut about the sky falling, where "the sky falling" means the end of the world. It goes back to ancient Rome, "Fiat Justitia ruatcaelum," or "Let justice be done though the heavens fall," a phrase demonstrating the Roman concept of law enforcement. It was also used for the James Bond film *Skyfall*.

and suffering. Still, he watches over Chise and hopes that she'll lay down her burden. Whether she does or not, she is free, regardless of what anyone says. Chise has been bound for some time, so he is attempting to show her how to free herself.

25 "That branch was born from the soil where the earth itself begins, and its path will someday lead it back to the heart of the stars."

The gjá that hides the dragons' aerie is a rare landform formed by the clashing of tectonic plates. This is where the earth begins, and where it sinks beneath the surface.

In a mythological sense, that connects to the interstice where Nevin and Chise currently stand.

In terms of Iceland's history, this is also where the world's first democracy was born—the starting place of the country itself.

26 "It will always light your way, wherever you choose to walk."

22 "I wish that you might take a little more pride in yourself."

The way to save someone who's lost in the maze of self-debasement is to help them understand their value. Perceiving their own worth gives them confidence and pride.

23 "My thanks. [My name] was a gift from Lindel. I think it's rather splendid."

Names are a means of expressing one's self. To have pride in your name is to have pride in yourself.

24 "You are free."

Most people are free, including their choice of how to live—even if the choice is between living with a curse and breaking it.

Chise is certainly free to continue harboring a curse someone placed on her, but Nevin would be happier if she freed herself of that burden. But he chooses to remind her that she is free, rather than directly stating that hope. Nevin is well aware that freedom can bring both release

 "I really appreciate your help with my wand, and that you let me stay here."

Chise expressing gratitude for the bed and food.

A reminder that the root word for Chise's name comes from the Ainu word "ciset," which roughly means "the place where we sleep."

Meanwhile, in Chise's shadow, Ruth is hastily packing their luggage.

31 "Everything is connected. I can go anywhere."

Nevin gave Chise the push she needed, and she takes his words literally. She finally believes that this is what she wants.

So she makes a wish.

A wish is the root of the magic in this world, and by tapping her wand to the ground she can borrow the power of the planet itself. This gesture is the same one Elias used when he chanted a travel spell back in chapter 1, so perhaps she's unconsciously trying to move the way he did.

A staff (wand) provides support to a traveler.

Nevin speaks to Chise through a wand made from himself, pushing her forward.

 "Every soul's journey will eventually end here, and one day begin again."

"Here" being the interstice. Those that live will die and cross this boundary line, and either be reborn and set out on a new life's journey or vanish into the distance.

28 "For now, we must part."

Dragons like Nevin have a very circular worldview. He is saying that when Chise dies, they will meet here again.

29 Chise Returns from the Vision

In most stories of visions, when you wake from the vision you find very little time has passed.

The visions are created by your mind all at once, with all information provided at the instant of their creation and packed densely into that moment.

The Japanese calls her a wolverine, an omnivore of the Mustelidae family that lives in chilly areas like the taiga and tundra. Through fairly small, it is known to be exceedingly violent. The English name "wolverine" means "like a wolf." That reputation for violence is upheld by the superhero of the same name.

The wolverine looks like a cross between a weasel and a tanuki. They run about 65-105 cm long and weigh around 10 kg, so they're not particularly large. They normally eat small animals, bird eggs, animal corpses, and fruit, but when starvation threatens they become ferocious, attacking deer, sheep, or even moose that are much larger than them. To do so, the wolverine drops from trees onto their prey's back, destroying the spine with their powerful jaws, and either buries the body in the snow or drags it up into the tree to eat a piece at a time.

35 "I could go anywhere."

Transformed into a bird of fire, Chise flies directly south. The power of her emotions makes her journey swift.

32 "You wanna go?"

The fire sprites. so common in Iceland, hear her wish and come to help.

33 "We'll circle the world on wings of flame!"

What Chise transforms into looks like a phoenix. A phoenix is a bird of fire, and when its life runs its course, it burns itself and is reborn. This legend may have originated with the Egyptian god Bennu.

Bennu was a bird that served the sun god Ra. It was reborn with the rising sun each day, and flew into the fire and died each night. This story spread across Europe, linked to the story of the resurrection of Jesus Christ. In ancient Greece, people began connecting it to fire spirits like the salamander and the phoenix, embellishing their legends. While there is a phoenix on Solomon's list of 72 demons, this was a creation after the fact.

34 "She may be far more willful than I suspected."

38 "I'm not feeling inspired to do anything."

Much as at the start of chapter 18, we have a rare glimpse into Elias' mind.

At times like these, an English gentleman may try working in the garden, but since Chise has taken over all that work, he's reluctant to interfere.

39 "And what did that old busybody tell her?"

If a fiancée gets taken out to the country, all the beans on childhood secrets get spilled. Elias may be unaware of that cliché, but he's certainly revealing a lot about himself here.

40 Elias and the Bird of Fire

Just as Chise wished, she flew straight to Elias.

One source of inspiration for Kore Yamazaki was a fantasy novel by Cliff McNish called *The Doomspell*, which also contains a scene in which the heroine, Rachel, is able to fly due to the strength of her feelings.

36 "There's only one place I want to go."

Definitions of magic vary from one fantasy to another, but sometimes it's simply a means to know yourself.

37 Centaur

Half-human, half-horse creatures from Greek mythology. "Centaur" is an anglicized version of "Kentaur." The origin is believed to be the first sightings of mounted Scythians—a terrifying sight to Greeks, who had no custom of riding horses.

While centaurs were skilled with bows and spears and quite barbaric, they also produced wise men like the sage Chiron.

Within this series, we see centaurs like this one blending into modern society.

London to his home, he used Chise's magic, but this is ten times that distance. That would have been enough to leave Chise vomiting blood and collapsing before.

44 "But...I had my wand... Thought I'd be okay..."

Thanks to faerie assistance and the power of her wand, Chise was able to work the spell, but relying too heavily on those things can be dangerous.

45 "There are so many things I want to say to him..."

Chise and Elias' relationship is deepened not through words but actions, but she still wishes to put it in words.

46 "She's warm..."

Calling back to the "cold" Elias felt in chapter 17. While he may not have the right words for it, feelings like this clearly demonstrate what lies between the two of them.

41 "I *meant* to use the spell you cast to bring me here originally."

Chise was trying to replicate the transportation spell Elias used in chapter 1, even though she needed to cover ten times the distance.

42 "I asked the neighbors for help."

She performed this spell not with her own power but by properly borrowing power from the neighbors.

By making sure to explain that, Chise is being more talkative than she's been until now, and Elias responds not with words but with an embrace. In this moment, their relationship subtly shifts.

43 "There, see?! Have you any notion of how far it is from here to the aerie? Using magic to fly from there to here was unutterably foolish!"

Approximately 1800 km, or three hours on an airplane. When Elias flew from this staff. Once, while on an errand to Arcadia, Hermes found two snakes fighting, and when he threw the staff between them, they ceased to struggle, twining themselves around the staff instead. Ever since, the image of a winged staff with two snakes wrapped around it has become a common icon, also called Caduceus. A symbol of peace, it is also used by many merchant organizations.

Meanwhile, on the alchemy side, Hermes was equated with the Egyptian god of knowledge, Thoth, referred to as Hermes Trismegistus, while the Romans called him Mercury, linking him to the element of the same name. Because of that, the two snakes around his staff are often said to represent sulfur and mercury, a demonstration of the base elements in alchemy.

Sometimes the wands themselves hold great magical power. The little gold rod that appears in Nibelungenlied is said to have the power to make its wielder the ruler of all humanity.

All around the world, canes have been used to make walking easier, so they were symbols of protection and guidance for travelers. Staffs were also a symbol of male virility, and many regions associate them with plenty or with royal authority.

Making a Magic Wand

So how does one go about making a magic wand?

When the wand is a gift from a god, it is

DISCUSSION 2: The Making of a Magic Wand

Inspired by Chise making herself a magic wand in volume 4, we'd now like to examine the history of magic wands and the ways in which they are made. For an explanation of the types of wands, see *Supplement I*, page 48, "Magic Wands."

Magic Wands

Since days of yore, sages, mages, and those who act on the behalf of gods have wielded magic wands, staves, or rods.

In the Old Testament Book of Exodus, God gave Moses and his brother Aaron a rod known as Aaron's Rod, which they used to bring plagues upon Egypt. This rod transforms itself into a snake to frighten the Pharaoh. Water touched by the rod turns into blood, and all the fish within die. It calls forth plagues of frogs, lice, flies, and locusts. It brings disease and hail. Finally, Moses raises the rod when he parts the Red Sea.

In Greek mythology, Asclepius, the god of medicine, carried a staff wrapped in a snake. He used the power of this staff to heal the sick and bring the dead back to life.

Similar to Asclepius's staff, and often confused with it, is Caduceus, the staff carried by Hermes, the messenger of the gods. Apollo, god of the sun, gave Hermes

The intended use of a wand will change the size and materials, but Elias uses a wand almost a meter long to assist with his spells, and where needed, is prepared to fight with it or use it as a walking aid.

Selecting Materials

Magic wands are generally made of wood, due to the need for manageable weight and sturdiness. In modern times one could certainly look into harder plastics or lightweight metalwork, but to transmit magic and for use as an extension of a mage's own body, natural materials are preferable.

Another advantage of natural materials is that by choosing a tree with history, the mythological significance of that wood is incorporated into the resulting wand. As shown in these chapters, the wood itself brings meaning with it, and a wand made from it is imbued with that power. With Celtic tree worship, the symbolism and associations are critical, and these differ for each type of tree.

For example, rowan is a tree dedicated to the Irish goddess Brigid, so it's a symbol of plenty, craftsmanship, and fire, and protects the body from temptation and disease. On top of that, it's a sign of the earth's energy and can protect one from evil spirits of the deceased.

However, as we mention with the holly in chapter 25, this symbolism can vary from place to place. The significance of a tree varies according to the lives of those

often a part of that god or a fragment of its power on loan. For example, Aaron's rod from the Old Testament is itself one of God's miracles, carrying destructive force as powerful as anything from the Book of Revelation, and visiting retribution for the suffering inflicted on the Israelites by the Egyptians.

But in *The Ancient Magus' Bride*, wands are tools created by mages to aid with their work. As explained several times already, magic in this series is a "prayer" or a "miracle," and while performing magic is possible without a wand, wands are extremely helpful both in clarifying the intended effect and stabilizing the flow of magic power.

One easy comparison might be the laser pointers (or physical pointers) teachers use to direct students' attention to the blackboard. Magic wands are useful in much the same way. The magic wands seen in the *Harry Potter* series are often thin, and about 50 cm long; they're of little practical use as a walking aid or weapon, but are very good for detailed marking of the spell target.

In magic circles, a magical tool used like this is often called a focus (pl. foci).

Making a staff involves several steps. Depending on the school of magic, the details may vary, and many involve additional rituals to allow the use of magic, so there's no simple way to describe the process. However, within *The Ancient Magus' Bride*, it generally involves planning, finding materials, creation, and the infusion of magic.

The Ancient Magus' Bride, it's traditional for the finishing touches to be applied by a mage's master, giving the wand even more power. Passing it to their master's hands strengthens the wand's ability to support the mage, but it's also done because the process of infusing an artifact with magic is not an easy one. These finishing touches often involve parts of the apprentice's flesh (hair or blood), gemstones with magical power, or plant matter with history. Hair, blood, or other parts of the wielder's flesh are used to strengthen the connection to the mage, making the wand a part of themselves. The auras of the mage and the wand should be one and the same.

A Mage's Initiation

Including the wand-making arc, the events that take place in Iceland are essentially an initiation that enhances Chise's abilities as a mage. Cultures the world over have initiation rituals, often performed when a child becomes an adult, but for mages, they're critical for development.

Chise became an apprentice mage when Elias purchased her, but Elias is part of no magic society in particular, treats her as family, and rarely discusses magical theory or explains what things mean. Instead, he directs her to use her Sight and perform a purification. This has a positive impact on her mental state, but it also results in her throwing magic around without having learned to adjust her perspective from that of an ordinary person

around it, and this, in turn, means feelings about it vary. In *The Ancient Magus' Bride*, magic is both a prayer and a miracle, but its fundamental nature is that of a negotiation with the natural laws of the world. But these laws don't exist in isolation. They're created by the natural environment, culture, emotions, and lives in the vicinity, all of which have a strong influence on the world around them. The symbolism is a clue to unraveling these relationships.

In Chise's case, by using wood from the linden that grew from the dragon Nevin's body, she has given her wand a magical bond and power, including the vision she has of him.

Magical Infusion and Artificing

Once it's time to actually make the wand, it's time for crafting skills, especially woodcarving. The wood itself must be shaped into the right form for a magical tool. This can only be done via the mage's own manual labor. By directly placing their hands on the wood and carving it, the wand and the wielder's auras connect, mingle, and merge. This creation process is referred to as artificing. Items that have magic power are called artifacts, and artificing is the process of creating artifacts. In Chise's case, by pouring herself into the work, she learns how to make use of magic power and experiences something closely akin to meditation.

This creation process gives Chise's wand quite a lot of power, but in the world of to that of a mage, while she's still ignorant of key magic principles.

This is a concerning state of affairs, as we see when Angelica worries about Chise's ignorance. Then Lindel, an experienced mentor, invites Chise to Iceland and gives her a chance to encounter her higher self. This initiation is a key part of her magical training, and vital to any mage who must connect to the world's laws.

The first time she went to Iceland, Chise had contact with the dragons and fell into the water. Passing through that ritual "death" and returning to life elevated her nature as a mage. This second time, she falls into the water once more, and this time she sees "something huge"—the water dragon—and begins to see the true scale of what the world has to offer. Later on, she'll be plunged into water again in the land of the faeries, experiencing another symbolic death that helps her overcome her past.

During the process of making her staff, Chise enters something like a meditative trance. Repetitive simple gestures infused with her desires polish the wand, carrying her to a place of selflessness that finally allows her to view herself objectively.

The instant she touches the completed staff, she has a vision of herself in conversation with Nevin, giving her the opportunity to reevaluate herself. He gives her the push she needs to take the next step forward, the power to act. Nevin's wand supports her not just physically and magically but also mentally.

CHAPTER **19** It is a long lane that has no turning.

SUMMARY

Back with Elias, Chise awakens from a dream in which her parents and little brother were all laughing together.

She finds two days have passed since she returned from the dragons' aerie. She and Elias begin shearing woolybugs, but mixed in with them is a snowbug, which attacks her to steal her body heat. As she warms up in the greenhouse, Chise tells Elias what she heard in Iceland, but when she touches on the "eating people" thing, he tries to erase her memories.

Chise explains how much these memories mean to her, and how important Elias has become. When Elias learns from her that what he felt was "loneliness," he appoints her his "teacher of human ways."

General Remarks

This chapter is a sort of intermission between major storylines, depicting daily life at Elias' home. But at the same time, it's about the growing emotions both Chise and Elias experienced during the wand-making arc and how that strengthened their bond. In chapter 18 Chise was bursting with things she wanted to say, but fell asleep instead. So now, when she and Elias start conversing, she tries to act on her desire to talk. The two of them uncover a conflict between Chise's feelings and Elias' thoughts, but overcoming that strengthens their relationship.

This chapter is also noteworthy for how Chise has begun to face her past head-on.

Chapter Title

It is a long lane that has no turning" is an English expression meaning that no matter how much misfortune or unhappiness we have, sooner or later things will take a turn for the better. These are words of encouragement when faced with an unpleasant job or a frustrating series of events.

In Japanese, we have similar expressions, like "Wait and the sea lanes will clear" (and "Wait and the nectar will flow").

In the context of this chapter, it can be taken to mean that changes eventually come to any path and that you will eventually find a place to rest.

4 Title Page

Chise awakens and looks out her window to find the air full of woolybugs.

5 "These things gathering outside your window are what inspired your dream."

These flying sheep are magical creatures linked to slumber. Their wool can be used in pillows or beds that encourage deeper sleep, or as an ingredient in sleep medicines.

6 "It's shearing time."

A common sight in English sheep pastures. In spring, all the sheep are sheared, making it easier for them to enjoy the summer.

7 Ruth's Behavior

Sheepdogs act to keep the flock in line. Ruth is circling the flock of woolybugs, guiding their movements.

8 Shears

Large scissors used for shearing sheep. They're also useful with woolybugs.

1 "Try not to act frightened. If it sees that you're afraid, it'll come closer."

In fantasy stories, it's quite common for aberrations like this one to feed on the fear they cause. Fear makes them stronger, so it lures them closer.

This is the first time we see Chise's mother looking normal. She's giving Chise good advice, with clear strategies for dealing with the "scary thing," and the whole family is together. Chise feels protected.

2 "That's a good girl, Chise."

Praise from her mother.

Chise's lived with her "curse" for so long that memories of happy days like this were buried deep in the back of her mind.

3 "Mom was there, and she wasn't crying. She wasn't mad at me."

The curse colored Chise's memories so strongly that she no longer remembered anything else.

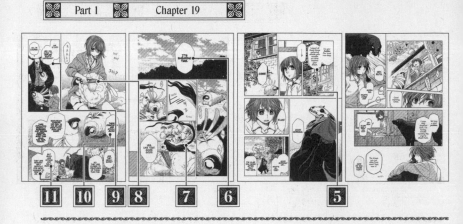

for producing a white waxy substance. The apple aphid is perhaps the most famous variety in Japan. When flying, these insects resemble not only cotton or wool but also snow. The sight of them flying around like powder snow is said to be a sign that the snowy season has arrived, so they're also called snowbugs.

11 "Much like wyrms and salamanders, they are remarkably difficult for most humans to perceive or find."

Salamanders are fire spirits that live within flame—not to be confused with the amphibians of the same name.

"Wyrm" is a general term for magical creatures with long thin bodies and no legs, covering everything from worms to snakes. Many are extremely large, including such legless dragons as Lindwurms and the Jörmungandr.

Magical creatures like this are much more similar to living beings than they are to faeries, and like living things, sustain themselves by feeding. But as they're

Blade shears are an ancient type of scissors, where two blades are squeezed together. These date back as far ancient Egypt and are also called "spring scissors." They reached Japan in the 6th century, imported from China.

Ordinary modern scissors use a pivot to connect two pieces of metal, and the cut is made when the opposing edges slide together.

9 "Are you going to explain what's happening?"

Chise is finally able to ask questions!

10 "These creatures are woolybugs."

Woolybugs are an original creation for this series. They consume cold and bring on the summer.

The Japanese name, "watamushi" (or "cotton bug," though the fictional and real-life insect use different kanji for "mushi"), is that of an insect of the Aphididae family that flies around like tufts of cotton in winter. They're known

that sound similar are inherently related and can be linked via sympathetic magic. What is a mere game to an ordinary human can be a tool of power to a mage.

[14] "They are often invoked before divining dreams, and they may help one experience a specific desired dream."

A method of fortune-telling based on the contents of dreams. A famous example in Japan is the New Year's dream, where the following are the most auspicious things to dream about: 1. Mt. Fuji, 2. Hawks, 3. Eggplants.

Dreaming is common to all humans, so there are dream-based divinations the world over. Dreams carry warnings and prophecies, and there are many reports of dreams of higher dimensions.

With magic in this series, dreams are often deeply related to the dreamer's psyche and to the laws of the world. You could consider them a type of second sight, but they aren't as concrete.

In Jungian and Freudian psychology,

found in extremely specific locations and dwell slightly out of phase with humans, it's rare for humans to notice them.

[12] "One sheep, two sheep…"

An English custom known as counting sheep. When you can't sleep, counting sheep is said to help you drift off. This may have started with shepherds who found themselves getting sleepy while counting a great number of sheep, or perhaps it's based on the similarities between the words "sheep" and "sleep." Since simple, tedious actions do make us sleepy, some people find it fairly effective.

[13] "You mustn't take children's rhymes lightly. Even simple wordplay can hold power."

"Wordplay" refers to taking words that sound similar and toying with the differences in meaning for witty results, as when two words have similar sounds but very different meanings or when two related words are swapped for comic effect.

From a magical perspective, words

After bathing in Ruth's fire breath, the snowbug grows slightly larger. If we think of it in game terms, this isn't just Null Fire—this is Absorb Fire.

The wand strike earlier was also ineffective; Chise's wand's element is red like the sun and the earth, both sources of heat. As was already mentioned, the wool cushions the blows, so bash damage is ineffective.

18   ZLOOORP

This tube is an ovipositor, which insects and whatnot use for laying eggs. An egg emerges and hatches immediately into offspring.

19   Charging Chise

The snowbug has acquired the heat needed to reproduce, but along with Chise's body heat, it likely absorbed fragments of her magic. It was probably drawn to her nature as a sleigh beggy as well as a heat source.

dreams are analyzed and used to diagnose a patient's mental condition, but that's analysis, not divination.

15   "What *is* this thing? It's cold!"

As will be explained later, this is a snowbug. Its nature is the opposite of the woolybug, and it eats warmth (absorbing heat).

As a result, its body feels extremely cold, to the point where even touching it feels like you're going to freeze.

The KRAK sound effect right after this is the cracking sound ice makes when it's flash-frozen.

16   "Darn! It didn't work!"

The blow from her wand is cushioned by the sheep-like wool. A mist sprang up around the wand, freezing part of it, and the frost spreads as far as Chise's hand.

17   "Fire doesn't work, either…?!"

Black Dogs are magical canines that can breathe fire like Hellhounds. Ruth doesn't often get to show it, but his combat capability is impressive!

similar to but the opposite of woolybugs. They primarily consume heat from sleeping humans and the embers of fires.

22 "It must have eaten some of your body heat."

Chise has entered a state of hypothermia and is unable to move. It's highly likely that the snowbug stole some of her magic as well, and Chise has never been terribly strong, so here she is shivering and confused.

Normally, hypothermia is caused when the body's temperature drops after exposure to cold, interfering with a number of bodily functions and causing the afflicted to feel unwell. The oxygen inside the body has an ideal temperature range and becomes less efficient below the normal internal temperature range (36-37 degrees Celsius).

Mild cases of hypothermia lead to shivering, sleepiness, and diarrhea, but more advanced cases can cause confusion and internal problems, eventually leading to paralysis of the heart and freezing to death due to multiple organ failures.

20 "You've had your chance to reproduce. Now off with you."

Spirits, faeries, and magical creatures that are physical manifestations of particular elements came into existence—at least in part—to explain natural phenomenon, including the changing of the seasons and various weather conditions.

Snowbugs are magical creatures that eat (absorb) heat to reproduce, representing the air chilling as winter approaches. Do you see snowbugs around as it gets colder, or does winter chill arrive because the snowbugs eat all the heat? Snowbugs and woolybugs are polar opposites, and so are their effects.

Elias tells it, "Off with you" because, as a magical creature, it has some limited understanding of human speech. But his words here are also charged with magical power meant to drive it away.

21 "A snowbug."

This explanation now seems belated, but as Elias tells Chise, these creatures are

Sadly, there are few suggestions that Elias himself is warm, so his touch is unlikely to warm anyone—or at least the idea has not occurred to him.

25 "Both of them gave me the push I needed."

Chise understood their intentions and is trying to move her relationship with Elias forward, but Elias himself remains unaware of this.

26 "Did I look tasty to you?"

She asks this because of things she was told during the wand-making arc. She finds herself wanting to ask Elias about having eaten humans, and decides to take that step.

27 "Chise! That is a story that you do not need to remember. Am I understood?"

Elias is attempting to cast a spell of forgetfulness. He believed that to maintain his relationship with Chise, he would have to erase these memories to keep her from fearing him.

23 "We must get the chill out of her bones."

Treating hypothermia involves warming the body inside and out, through things like wrapping the victim in blankets and taking them somewhere warm, while also giving them something hot to drink and massaging their hands and feet to improve circulation. If blood vessels contract and heat fails to spread through the body, it places a significant burden on the digestive system. It's critical to raise their temperature and restore normal bodily functions as soon as possible. Alcohol can be temporarily effective, but it also increases the rate at which heat is lost, so many times it backfires.

24 "Are you all right?"

To warm Chise, Elias has taken her to the conservatory and gathered woolybugs around her, using their body heat to warm her.

It's not shown all that often, but the Ainsworth residence grows a number of plants year-round in this conservatory.

30 "Am I not terrible and frightening to a human?"

A glimpse back to Elias when he lost control after Cartaphilus' chimera wounded Chise. Monstrous, yes, but it also reveals his rage when he sees her hurt. For Chise, that moment inspired something quite different from fear.

Since Chise has seen apparitions since she was very little, his external appearance alone is not enough to scare her. She was still able to understand most of his behavior, and he treated her like family.

31 "I used to have a family."

This is the first time Chise has ever talked about her family with Elias.

She's been trapped by the curse her mother placed on her and has been unable to talk about them calmly.

32 "My parents both had the sight, like me. And they were so in love with each other."

"Am I understood?" is not a request for permission but a demand. Chise has long suffered under demands like this, and she doesn't want to submit to them anymore. That's what leads her to knock the wand aside and shift the focus of his spell.

28 "No—!"

Chise finally has the strength to voice her refusal.

The flowers at the top of the page appear to be nasturtium. In flower language, nasturtium means "victory over suffering."

29 "It's a story about somebody I care about! I—! I don't *not* need it…"

Chise speaks plainly about their relationship.

"Yikes, momentum can sure go scary places fast…! So embarrassing!" she thinks, but she had to speak up.

Many faeries and non-humans hold this opinion of humans. Many of them can only perceive a lie once a promise is broken, so they've become wary of humans, believing them to be liars.

 "I don't know how to empathize with humans. Even if I wished to say the same words back to you, they would be lies."

Elias is a mage, but not human. He doesn't share human emotions or logic and therefore can't empathize with them. But he can tell when he's chosen the wrong words.

 "I can recite these facts. They are things I know."

What Elias says here sounds like something an AI might say. They have inputs and outputs and can diligently collect and analyze information, but that process is mechanical and based purely on logic. Since the fundamental basis for their decision-making never changes, they can't understand human emotions.

When Chise was little, both of her parents could see what she did. They protected her and the family was happy.

Before, Chise wouldn't have been able to talk about this part of her past at all.

 "But they all left me behind. They didn't want me with them."

The true root of Chise's trauma.

"That's why I decided I didn't want a family anymore."

A defensive reaction to prevent her trauma from being triggered further.

"When he talked about the future, I was always there. I was always part of it. I started to think I might actually have a future...as long as I was with him."

Not just the present. Sharing a future gave her hope.

"Humans lie."

43 **"I look forward to further lessons, teacher of human ways."**

Here Chise and Elias become each other's teachers. Their relationship is now less one-sided.

44 **"A few interesting birds flew by, but that was all."**

The messenger sent from the college—not a living bird, but a magical tool made from a bird's corpse.

45 **The pot in the conservatory**

A feather lies in the pot, shown here in close-up. The bird sent by the college was destroyed and buried here in secret.

The fact that Elias hid it yet left evidence behind may be another indication that he's still a child, and it shows a trace of the inhumanity that remains within. Perhaps the conservatory itself represents his state of mind.

39 **"Really?"**

As a unique creature, Elias has never experienced having someone of his own kind react differently than he would.

40 **"What name would you give to that feeling?"**

This isn't a thought experiment. He wants to know Chise's opinion.

41 **A Drop of Water and Ripples**

The word "loneliness" overlies this imagery because this is something Chise is also telling herself. Loneliness is an emotion she'd sealed away inside herself. Hearing this word sends ripples through Elias' heart, leading him to the discovery of a new emotion.

42 **"I thought so. He really is still practically a child."**

Chise is beginning to understand him.

SUMMARY

Chise has returned to her normal routine with Elias, spending time writing letters to people she knows and learning magic. But from time to time, Elias receives visitors that are not human.

One of these visitors is an ancient creature known as Ashen Eye, here to appraise Chise and gift her with a fur that transforms her into a fox.

Chise races out across the fields in fox form, but when Elias comes after her, she remembers him, and returns to human form.

Then the leannán sídhe arrives, stricken with worry over Joel's health.

CHAPTER 20

East, west, home's best.

General Remarks

This chapter is composed of mini-episodes depicting the daily routine at Elias' home, a number of different faeries, and some of the strange beings that Elias socializes with.

Meanwhile, one of these non-humans, Ashen Eye, provides a trial that deepens the emotional connection established in chapter 19. Ashen Eye gives Chise a fur that turns her into a fox. Chise runs out across the field in fox form, but remembers Elias and returns home, once again bringing the series back to the theme of "home" and what that means to us.

The introduction of Ashen Eye lays the foundation for the Yule arc that takes up the majority of volume 6, and the chapter ends with a lead-in to the leannán sídhe arc that kicks off volume 5.

Chapter Title

"East, west, home's best" is an English saying meaning that no matter how far from home you go, there's no place better. It's similar to chapter 24's title, "There's no place like home," which expresses the joy found in returning home. The concept of home is one of the series' primary themes.

Another similar expression is "A man's home is his castle." This comes from a ruling by the 16-17th-century English judge Sir Edward Coke, in which he declared, "For a man's house is his castle, et domus suacuiqueesttutissimum refugium [and each man's home is his safest refuge]," in *The Institutes of the Laws of England*.

someone, which is a good sign that she's started being able to talk about herself.

4 GWUMM GWUMM

A front-loading washing machine. The mage's house may have a faerie who does the housework, but there's some surprisingly high-tech machinery present.

5 "A gremlin!"

A type of faerie that began appearing in England in modern times. During the First World War, there was a lot of mechanical trouble with planes and whatnot, and it was attributed to strange creatures called gremlins. They're known to look like goblins with wings. In this series it looks more like a rabbit, and due to gremlins' association with aircraft, this one is wearing aviator goggles and a period flight jacket.

6 The Goat Guest

A goat head is often associated with the Christian devil Baphomet or Leonard, the devil summoned during the Sabbat.

1 "You're such a lazybones today, Joel!"

The elderly are known to often be early risers.

This is because they produce less melatonin, the hormone that encourages sleep. While they have trouble sleeping for long hours, they also grow tired easily, so it's natural to fall into an "early to bed, early to rise" routine.

2 Title Page

Chise studying magic. Has she removed her shoes because she was raised in Japan and hasn't broken the habit?

Here she's chipped some beeswax with a knife and is melting it in a beaker, making a magical medicine. Meanwhile, steam rises from another pot.

Ruth watches over her. On the bed lie a woolybug and an aethonic (a type of salamander).

3 "Hello there."

Chise is trying to write a letter to

human, that doesn't mean you're seeing their true form. Either this spell is strong enough to override Chise's Sight or the being itself is a higher-level one.

9   "Peer at it through your amulet."

According to legend, peering through stones hollowed out by the river current will allow you to see faeries. It lets you pierce the veil of illusion.

10   Purple

In Europe, purple was only attainable with a valuable dye made from a sea snail, so it was an extremely expensive color. In ancient Rome, it was a color used only the emperor.

11   "Up on the second floor, there's a locked closet."

The door is sealed with magic. It only opens when the need arises. This is a Western variant on Japanese legends about strange houses that bestow riches on those who happen across them—a room that only responds when asked by the home's owner.

Baphomet is a hermaphroditic devil with the head of a mountain goat, attended by witches, with whom he regularly copulates.

The origins of this diabolic image lie in the half-goat god Pan from Greek mythology, the horned god Cernunnos worshiped by the Druids, or a number of different half-beast Egyptian gods, all of which tended to be viewed as devils by Christians. Additionally, the Jewish religion (mother of Christianity) rose up among nomadic tribes with a strong taboo against bestiality, which may be related.

But here, this is merely an ancient being that wears a goat's head as part of its surface appearance.

7   "Fellow in knowledge."

A way to address a friend who also studies magic.

8   "That looks like a goat to you?"

Many fae or inhuman things have a spell cast on them that changes their appearance. Even if they still don't appear

berry flowers is said to be effective against laryngitis.

Syrups are liquids made with concentrated sugars. They're often mixed with herbal extracts to make the medicine easier to drink. It's common to water them down and drink them like juice.

16 **"Mmm, that's good. It tastes just as it did that day."**

Chise's pleased that she's learned to make it taste like Elias' medicine.

17 **"Wow, making fairy ointment is a *lot* of work."**

Fairy ointment is a magical substance that allows anyone to see faeries. The main ingredient is four-leaf clover, and it can be made either as an oil or an ointment.

When rubbed on the eyelids, it has the effect of canceling magic, removing the glamours that usually hide the fae and allowing humans to see what was hidden. This power is also known as the second sight, and the ointment is made for changelings without the Sight, or to allow

12 **"It opens only when Elias asks me to fetch things from it for him, and somehow, whatever I'm there to get is always exactly where I look first. It sure is strange."**

According to the author, the house itself has a consciousness, opening and closing doors at the will of its master and moving objects around. As shown in chapter 24, Silky can consult the house and change its interior design.

13 Ding Ding Diiiiing

The Ainsworth house sells home remedies, and the sales window is next to the front door. Customers ring the doorbell for service.

14 Simon

The local priest who monitors Elias. He has a chronic respiratory disease and relies on Elias' medicine.

15 **"Tea with elderberry syrup."**

A deciduous shrub. An extract from elder-

Then you add the seasonal flower and the four-leaf clover, and expose it to moonlight through windows to the east, west, north, and south, applying the power of all four cardinal directions.

Four-leaf clover are rare, so they alone have the power to disrupt deceptive spells. Finding one and wearing it on your head is also said to allow you to see faeries, and such clovers are especially effective when found before sunrise.

> **18** **"'Magic' is when we do something by borrowing power from faeries and spirits. It's strong enough to interfere with the laws of nature. Trying to use it without knowing or respecting the risks involved can have serious consequences."**

The core principles of magic within *The Ancient Magus' Bride*. Interfering with the laws of nature and borrowing power alone can all too easily end tragically.

As shown in this panel, trees growing out of books aren't an unusual sight.

half-human, half-faerie children to see. As an extension of that idea, in this series it becomes an ointment with the power to let any human see faeries.

As an example of legends about the fairy ointment, look at Andrew Lang's *The Lilac Fairy Book* (the 12th volume) and the story called "The Fairy Nurse." In this story, a midwife called to a faerie's house is given a green ointment to rub on the newborn baby. When she accidentally rubs some on her own eyes, she sees the faerie house for what it really is, and discovers a farmer's wife who was stolen away to be the faeries' wet nurse. The nurse rescues the stolen wife and reunites her with her farmer husband.

This panel touches on the creation of such an ointment, so let's elaborate on that.

Gold is put in water because gold is a perfect material, and its power purifies the water. Chemically speaking, gold is extremely stable and doesn't react when placed in water, but in magic circles, gold has considerable power.

The light of the moon when close to full also has a lot of magical power.

Now, if we're talking gods who had ash-colored eyes, the Greek goddess Athena is often called "Glaukopis Athena," translated as either "bright-eyed" or "gray-eyed." She was frequently associated with owls, and "Glaukopis" could also mean she had an owl's eyes.

The striped cloth and multiple bracelets remind one of some African tribes, and there is a theory that Athena originated in Africa. See *Black Athena* for details.

22 "I thought to call upon you and offer my blessings."

In European legends, local gods and witches would often appear at the births of children or coming-of-age ceremonies, offering blessings, curses, or augers. *Sleeping Beauty* is a prime example.

Originally this was a custom of having the local priest or priestess bless the baby and divine their future, and the stories sprang from that.

For similar themes, read the short story "The Sun and the Dead Alchemist" by Kiyomune Miwa, found in *The Ancient Magus' Bride: The Golden Yarn*.

19 "Hmm? You said you understood everything. If you always rely on notes, nothing will ever truly stick in your head."

Mages live long lives and often travel widely. Written notes can become a burden or are easily lost, so mages tend to focus on memorization. Alchemists take the opposite approach and prioritize leaving accounts of their techniques in writing.

20 "Your pardon for disturbing you so late."

The Japanese word for evening, "tasogare," sounds similar to words meaning "who is he?" Evening is a magical time where it can be difficult to identify those you encounter. Also known as "omagatoki," it is a time when the spirits are out and about.

21 "Ashen Eye!"

An ancient creature that has lived for millennia. Nothing is known about it but the name. We could perhaps hazard a guess that it came from a desert, since Chise mentions it smells like sand.

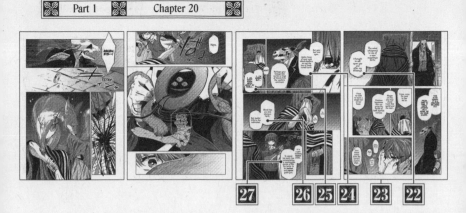

believed to be. Alternately, perhaps earth is linked with black in the five elements.

25 "I don't know much about my family."

Chise's father and brother left when she was quite young, and her mother is dead, so she grew up knowing very little about them.

26 "Blood ties are vital among a herd but matter little to the individual."

For those who live long lives and form no tribes (unlike humans), lineage is of little use. Ashen Eye has likely seen this first-hand countless times.

This phrasing reveals a lot about Ashen Eye's perspective. It is a creature several tiers above humans, and tends to view us the way we do pets.

27 "Far better to let instinct and nature guide you."

The stronger the fae, the more likely they are to find human intelligence vexing. Their feeling that it's best to live according to whatever impulse strikes one means that they often couch curses in the form of advice.

23 "Mages are the few that stand twixt this world and the next."

Translated here as "the next" is a word made from the kanji for "ghost" and "world," describing the world in which divine spirits dwell. This is contrasted with a commonly used word made from the kanji for "real" (or "present") and "world."

In Shinto, that first concept is known as "tokoyo"—"eternal" and "world"—where gods and spirits live forever, unchanging; this contrasts to the constant upheavals in the real world.

We saw Nevin speak of the real world and the world after death. This is Ashen Eye's version of that same concept.

24 "But your hair and eyes, unlike those of most such island-dwellers, are not the hue of fresh-turned earth."

Most Japanese have black hair and dark eyes, but Chise's hair has a reddish hue.

The concept of the earth being black comes from ancient Egypt, where the blacker the earth, the more fertile it was

people," a euphemistic term for fairies. Applying this word to humans with a particular nature and then redefining their distance from the world of magic with the choice of kanji shows off Kore Yamazaki's fantasy chops.

"I don't like the cold."

A rare expression of emotion from Elias.

At the end of the wand-making arc, Elias learned that this emotion was loneliness, but he still experiences it as if the house grows cold in Chise's absence.

Given the nature of his body, it seems unlikely that cold poses much of a problem for him, so this is purely an emotional response.

"It's a delight to watch the young grow up."

Ashen Eye has lived for thousands of years, so someone like Elias, who has lived only a few hundred, obviously must be nothing but a child. In much the same way, Lindel treats Elias like a child.

Ashen Eye may be like a cranky old woman who can't stop pulling pranks, but

"When at last you choose to rest, the field where you lay your head will be where you truly belong."

Losing her human form frees Chise from all the ties that bind her. Ashen Eye tells her to live free, to choose her own place.

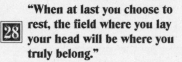 "Is your loathing of the humans with the eyes to see you truly so deep?"

The act of seeing a faerie means perceiving that faerie's form, and limits their actions accordingly. Being seen identifies them and subjects them to scrutiny, so ancient ones always hate being seen. In the Japanese, the verb "shibaru," or "bind," is used here in place of "see."

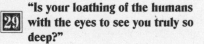 "Or have you forgotten that they, too, were once called our kindly neighbors?"

In the Japanese, "sleigh beggy" is given the kanji meaning "dearest child of the night." It was originally a Manx word for "little

36   "Without you here to teach me, I won't know what to do."

Elias has never put his feelings into words, so he lacks the vocabulary to do so when the moment comes, and ends up being very direct.

37   Nuzzle

Carnivores like foxes with long snouts often express affection by rubbing their noses.

38   "Lonely."

The word Chise taught him. By echoing what he learned from her, he is reminding her that she has more to teach.

certainly does not see its behavior as anything more than teasing the children.

33   "I was—wait. What was I again...?"

As Chise raced off across the fields in the form of a fox, the animal's instincts swallow her and her human identity blurs. Spells of this nature often lead to people forgetting what they really are.

34   "I hear someone calling me. Almost shouting in my ear."

The screams of her human mind don't reach Chise as she delights in running in her new form, but her familiar, Ruth, appears and questions her.

35   "Chise."

Having her name called is enough to restore her identity and human form. By answering the call, Chise recovers her human mind.

43 42 41 40 39

often called werewolves. The latter, victims of curses or spells that force them to become wolves, are called Lycanthropes, a popular belief throughout the sheep pastures of Europe. It's said to have been a mythological warning and explanation of the dangers of rabies.

42 "It can be convenient if you get the hang of it."

All over Europe, there are spells to transform into animals. The heroes in Norse mythology used bear-pelts to make themselves go berserk, after which they would attack friend and foe alike, fighting to the death.

Elias speaks entirely as if the fur is a magical item, but given the risk of being lost in the fur's spell, it's certainly one to use with caution.

43 "Ashen Eye's behavior was nothing short of kidnapping!"

The Japanese text indicates that Ashen Eye acted as it did entirely for its own enjoyment and amusement.

39 "Let's go home."

Chise and Elias finish things by emphasizing a return to their home, where they both belong.

40 "You were under something of a curse."

The effect of a curse limits your actions and thoughts via magical interference. It's quite common for the cursed to be unable to think or make decisions properly.

The were-curse cast on Chise shifted her thoughts to those of a fox, and even with the transformation lifted, she'll temporarily have trouble thinking like a human would.

41 "There are two distinct types: those who are naturally born with both human and bestial forms, and those humans who are cursed to take an animal's shape under certain conditions."

The former are shapeshifters, switching between human and wolf form. These are appearance to that of a wolf, and following the mechanisms of sympathetic magic—that similar-seeming things *are* the same thing—Chise is changed into something indistinguishable from the actual beast.

As an example of similar sympathetic magic, we have the berserkers from Norse mythology. The word "berserk" means "one who wears a bear's skin," and these fighters wore bearskins and fought with the strength of bears.

Why A Fox, Not a Wolf?

If she were European, perhaps she would just have become a wolf, but here we see the particular nature of sympathetic magic. Since sympathetic magic is all about the mind's eye, the power of imagination is required from both the caster and the castee.

Now, wolves in Japan went extinct over a hundred years ago, so Chise is not particularly familiar with them. So her mind went to similar animals, settling on the image of a fox. Since this is sympathetic magic, the castee's mental image affected the outcome of the transformation.

Wolves in Europe are sometimes positioned as field spirits, while Japanese foxes are associated with Inari, also a god of grains. Chise is a teenage girl and the ferocious strength of wild animals is not that appealing to her, so this transformation is more appropriate. The size of a fox compared to Elias' beast form is also fitting,

DISCUSSION 3: The Wolf's Skin: Man and Beast

The wolf's skin Ashen Eye gives Chise turns her into a fox, and she runs out across the fields.

What does it mean to become a beast?

Let's take a look at werewolves from both legendary and psychological standpoints.

Tales of Transformation

There are many tales of people becoming animals and of animals becoming people, and not just in Europe. They fall largely into the following categories.

Totem: Imagining the ancestors as animals, and transforming while under their protection. A facet of ancestor worship.

Sympathetic Magic: By imitating or eating a portion of a strong creature (a predator or an oversized or poisonous creature) that lives in the tribe's domain, they gain that creature's strength.

Origin Stories: Explanations for aspects of a particular creature, such as in Greek mythology's story of Arachne being transformed into a spider—an explanation for why spiders weave webs.

In this case, Chise using a pelt to transform is an example of sympathetic magic. The act of a person placing a wolf skin over themselves transforms their outward and on the night of the full moon could not be slain by ordinary bullets—there are notes suggesting the use of silver bullets instead.

Werewolves are often humanoid, but there are two types—those that physically transform into wolves, and those controlled by the spirit of a wolf. The latter type is referred to a possession, and often takes the form of a curse.

Possession by animal spirits was used to explain violent paroxysms, hysteria during pregnancy, pica, overeating, forms of borderline personality disorder, and sudden outbursts of violence.

In Slavic legends, this type of werewolf was called "vukodlak," and was closely linked to vampires and ghouls. Some stories say those killed by werewolves become vampires, or that vampires must first spend time being werewolves. Yet in other areas, werewolves and vampires are considered enemies. In those regions, when vampires encounter werewolves, only one leaves alive.

Shapeshifting as Astral Projection

Another concept related to lycanthropes is when witches take on the form of their familiar. Witches are able to eject their soul from their body, and that soul can take over the cat, wolf, or fox that serves as their familiar, allowing them to control it as they will. Also, souls that have left the body can take the form of a particular animal or mental image, a form of astral projection.

and we can't ignore the value of originality to any fantasy manga.

Werewolf Legends

Stories about werewolves or wolfmen are the most famous stories about people transforming into wolves. Tales like these are found nearly everywhere wolves live, but are especially popular in areas with large wolves, like the eastern wolf or the gray wolf, where wolves pose a serious threat. Even in Japan, the words for "wolf" and "great god" are homonyms, showing a tendency to elevate the wolf to divine status.

In English, people transformed into wolves are called either werewolves or lycanthropes. "Lycanthrope" comes from the Greek for wolf ("lykos") and human ("anthropos") while "werewolf" comes from ancient Germanic for human ("wer") and wolf ("wolf"). These and similar terms are used when humans turn into hairy beasts (mostly wolves). When that happens, the person loses their human mind, attacking and eating animals and humans—or even digging up corpses from graves.

Many legends have these transformations occur on the night of the full moon, and because moonlight brings madness, we have the word "lunatic" (where "luna" = "moon").

We have records dating from the 16th century saying that werewolves grew stronger with the waxing of the moon,

What's more, when Chise becomes a beast, follows her instincts, and runs out across the fields, Ashen Eye tells her that where her instincts take her is where her home is. This could be seen as a trial to determine the location of her home—a major theme of *The Ancient Magus' Bride*.

In her fox form, the first to speak to her is Ruth, her familiar (and other half), but he has his limits in that role—his first priority is her desires and impulses. Chise has forgotten that she is human, forgotten her home, and wants nothing more than to run forever. All Ruth can do is go with her.

But then Elias catches up, in his own beast form. He has access to Chise's shadow and can always appear from within it in his bone-headed human form (see the Black Dog arc), but instead he chooses to pursue her as a beast. With both wearing inhuman shapes, and with their hearts exposed, their emotions are unleashed. When they agree where their home lies, they return to human form. Chise (the Ainu word for "home") returns home as a human. Their hearts have passed another trial, and each of them grows as a result.

As Chise is a mage's apprentice, we could interpret it in that light, but as her very flesh is altered, animal possession seems more likely. Since her familiar, Ruth, is a Black Dog, perhaps it is only natural for her to shift into a similar form; perhaps her having a canine familiar is foreshadowing.

Why Did Chise Transform?

All investigations into the setting aside, we'd like to examine exactly why Ashen Eye brought forth a were-curse in chapter 20.

"Inhuman meets girl" in one of the Japanese taglines for *The Ancient Magus' Bride*, and that's a major part of the overall plot, as mentioned in *Supplement I*'s "Discussion 1: A Fantasy of Otherworldly Matrimony." Chise has learned of Elias' past, and the possibility that he was a man-eating monster, but has yet to take the next step forward from that. This is a story she's been told, but she doesn't have the concrete experience to allow her to fully understand it. But the removal of Chise's core humanity, transforming her to a beast that acts on pure instinct, can help clarify the relationship between her as a human and Elias as something *not*.

Two moments come to mind that illustrate this give-and-take: in chapter 23, where the faerie queen, Titania, says, "You'd serve her best by helping her shed her human trappings," or the scene where Chise and Elias kiss beneath the mistletoe in chapter 25, mimicking human customs.

The
Ancient Magus'
Bride
Supplement
II

Part 2

CHAPTER 21

Looks breed love.

SUMMARY

The leannán sídhe unexpectedly arrives to plead for help for Joel Garland, an elderly man who lives nearby and tends his rose garden. Chise rushes to Joel's house and finds him on his deathbed. Elias estimates he has a week left. This is due to both his advanced years and the fact that the leannán sídhe, a type of vampire, has been drawn to him, living in the same house and draining away his soul. The leannán sídhe insists she doesn't love him.

When Chise learns of Joel's condition she decides to make a fairy ointment for the two of them. It takes five days to make, and the faeries won't help her, so Elias warns that it will be difficult, but Chise decides to pursue it.

General Remarks

This storyline technically started at the end of chapter 20, but this chapter marks the true beginning of the fairy ointment arc. A leannán sídhe, who can only live by draining people's souls, was once drawn by the beauty of roses and fell in love with an old man named Joel Garland. Now, as Joel lies dying, Chise decides to try her hand at making the notoriously difficult fairy ointment.

Faced with this example of the tragedy so often brought by love between humans and non-humans, we see how Chise has grown and how Elias has changed.

Chapter Title

Looks breed love" is an English expression. Variants include "Love comes by looking," or "Love comes in at the eyes." People talk about loving the soul or the personality, but in fact, the moment you fall in love starts with finding their face, their body, their expressions, and their gestures all appealing—possibly even love at first sight. Love so often grows from a wonderful first impression.

In this story, a single moment of eye contact led to the leannán sídhe becoming trapped at Joel's side, tightly bound to him. This title points to the nature of her love.

Faeries and Vampires

To Japanese people, the word "yousei" conjures up adorable images of picture-book faeries. But the real ones, while occasionally helpful, were often quite harmful and something to be afraid of. They were often used to explain the inexplicable.

For example, the idea of vampires explained how an illness could abruptly weaken and kill someone, casting them as the victim of something supernatural. When a gifted, imaginative poet died young, it could be due to debauchery and the lifestyle led by many notorious creative people, but since many such poets also dreamed of beautiful women, the idea of the leannán sídhe, a faerie that loves poets, was born.

1 Chise's Clothes

She's slung that shoulder bag right over her pajamas. She didn't even stop to put on socks. It's clear she thinks the situation is urgent.

2 Title Page

Joel Garland and the leannán sídhe in happier days. She's simply floating nearby and watching over Joel as he tends to the garden. It's all she needs to be happy.

3 "Chise, get on!"

One can't ordinarily treat large dogs as mounts, but Black Dogs are certainly big enough to carry someone of Chise's weight.

7 "He's at death's door."

Mages have ways of perceiving someone's vitality. Examining an aura or astral body can give them a good idea of someone's health. Here, Joel's aura is fading, allowing Elias to predict his coming death.

8 "How unusual, seeing one of you attached to a human of such advanced age."

Leannán sídhe attach themselves to young poets, making their talent bloom while draining their lives. The poets they haunt produce masterpieces but die young. That inherent nature makes it unlikely that a leannán sídhe would target someone elderly.

9 "Once a parasite latches onto a host, the host's fate is sealed."

In this series, faeries are invisible to most humans. When a human is targeted by any type of parasite, such as a leannán sídhe, they have no way of resisting.

4 The Unlocking Spell

Chise taps the lock with her wand and addresses it, using words of magic to turn the lock as if applying oil. This spell involves imagining the lock opening, thus magically producing that result.

5 "Open to this golden key!"

An item from *Grimm's Fairy Tales*. In one of the stories, a boy finds a golden key in the snow and looks for an iron box to which it fits. The story ends by stating that the reader will have to wait until he opens it to find what treasures lie within.

In George MacDonald's version of *The Golden Key*, a boy finds a golden key at the end of a rainbow, a girl gets lost in the land of the faeries, and both set off on a journey to find the key's lock.

6 ZLIIIP

Elias is able to hide in and travel within people's shadows.

are, he does not realize how badly this will hurt the leannán sídhe.

12 "Elias!"

Oblivious to the mood, Elias keeps saying painful things until Chise explodes and cuts him off.

13 "What I feel for him is *not* love."

She tries to deny it, but it's a leannán sídhe's nature to love the opposite sex.

14 Chise's Jacket

Chise has Elias' jacket over her shoulders. He may have failed to read the room, but he has learned what a gentleman does at moments like these.

10 "All I wanted was to be near him!"

Parasitic fae frequently drain life through kisses or sexual intercourse—or by drinking blood—but even without those things, their ongoing presence near a human is enough to slowly drain the human's life away.

11 "Have you forgotten what you are?"

The special powers a magical being possesses are intrinsic to their own destiny. A leannán sídhe is a lover of poets, and as long as she remains a leannán sídhe, she will grant talent to the men her heart fancies and consume their lives in return.

Most magical creatures' lives are defined like this, just as a house spirit can't live without doing housework and a banshee must lament the dead.

Elias himself is something like a fae, and to him these fates are a clear and obvious law—one he can't help but point out. With his emotions as undeveloped as they

spread to the British Isles. The plain cross used in Christian sects is sometimes called the Latin or Roman cross (and has a longer lower arm), while the Celtic cross is surrounded by a circle, representing the sun.

According to Irish legend, when St. Patrick was trying to spread Christianity in Ireland, he combined the local symbol for the sun (and thus life) with the Latin cross.

Ever since, the Celtic cross has been a Christian symbol, and it's frequently used for gravestones. In recent years, with the rise of Celtic and Breton nationalism, it's been increasingly used as the symbol of political parties.

18 "Growing older and feeling death's approach is scary."

As the subsequent lines explain, it's not merely the fear of death itself but of being unable to do the things one used to be capable of—the fear of feeling your body fail and your mind struggle to keep up. Growing old can mean dementia or a

15 "Are you Death...?"

Europe has legends about being visited by the personification of death.

Called either Death or the Grim Reaper, this personification appears as a skeleton carrying a scythe. In the Celtic folklore that influences this series, there's a type of faerie named Ankou from the Brittany area of France that personifies this same idea.

16 A Warning

Elias doesn't hesitate to inform Joel that his life is coming to an end. We can assume Elias never considered trying to hide the fact, but it does look as if he at least attempted to find the right moment to break the news.

17 Gravestones

Celtic crosses like these are common in English graveyards. The Celtic cross is a symbol widely used in Ireland and Celtic areas of Great Britain, and is an old icon that existed long before Christianity

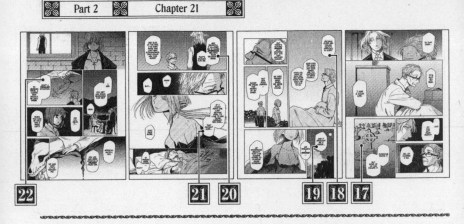

To him, she was a mirage he glimpsed a single time, and the strongest impression he retains in his heart is the color of her eyes. That moment is both the source of his love and the fragment of talent the leannán sídhe unwittingly bestowed upon him.

22 "What a peculiar situation."

Fae or spirits that prey upon humans rarely deviate from their nature. As a result, they feel indifferent to the deaths of humans. That's simply how they live. This entire situation, then, is very unusual.

The strangeness of it can be seen in the way the leannán sídhe sits by the bed, as well. When leannán sídhe are depicted, it is always a story of love, so the pair would be shown standing side by side or lying in bed together, or else with the leannán sídhe gazing down at their dying lover.

loss of emotional stability. Part of the fear of aging is feeling like you're no longer yourself.

19 "A vision, or a perhaps a mirage."

Joel admits that he's aware it might not have been real. The Japanese idiom used here mentions the "noon light." For more, see *Supplement I*, page 165.

20 "It allowed me to share afternoon tea with your delightful ward."

He's referring to Chise. In the Japanese, he compares her to a "new spring sprout," a metaphor for youth and the energy that comes with spring. For the elderly, contact with youth can be energizing.

21 "If I could make one last selfish wish, I'd love to see those currant-red eyes..."

At this point, Joel does not use the term "leannán sídhe," either because he doesn't know what she is or because he's unsure.

account and decides to allow her to take this step. Elias has begun to change, too.

27 "But you mustn't get carried away and exhaust yourself."

When Chise uses magic, she's unable to control the power, so she grows tired and collapses. The wand has increased her control, but vigilance is still called for.

28 "The jar is placed on a window-sill for a full day at each of the cardinal directions, that it may bathe in both moonlight and sunlight."

Just as with the creation of the wand, the magic of the celestial bodies can be applied to magical compounds. A day is spent gaining the power of the guardian spirit of each of the four directions: east, west, north, and south.

29 "They will not help you, no matter how you ask."

Mages borrow the power of faeries in order to interfere with the laws of nature,

23 "Is it okay if I make some?!"

Chise tells Elias her idea and asks his advice. This, too, is a step forward for Chise, and a shift in their relationship.

24 "As a general rule, the fae become very displeased when normal humans see them."

As the fae are normally invisible, being seen creates a link—a type of magical control.

25 "If they found you'd made some, they would be extremely cross."

A reminder of the scene in chapter 20, where Ashen Eye is described as hating those with the eyes to see [bind] them. Eyes that can see a faerie are also eyes that can restrict their actions.

26 "You've never pushed to get something you want before."

Elias is aware that this is the first time Chise has proposed a course of action, so he takes that significant development into

The
Ancient Magus'
Bride
Supplement
II

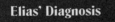

The way she cradles the ointment jar to her chest, as if it were an infant, feels maternal.

Elias' Diagnosis

The moment Elias lays eyes on Joel, he says, "What's happened to this fellow? He's at death's door."

How does Elias know Joel's condition without even laying a hand on him? It seems as if Elias is seeing something else entirely.

Spiritualists often claim to be able to see something called "auras," which depict the overall biological balance and life energy of the owner. Depending on the person and the health of their aura, its color and size can vary.

In this moment, Elias sees that Joel's life energy is withering, and thus knows he is at death's door.

We can assume that the leannán sídhe has been draining this aura.

but since Chise can't do that this time, she has to draw on her own magic. We saw the strain of this sort of thing in chapter 16, when Lindel used his own magic to hide himself and Elias beneath the forest veil—he started bleeding and then collapsed from exhaustion.

Since Chise has already spent days in bed just from using her Sight and performing a purification, we know that this could well put her life in danger.

30 Hands That Don't Quite Touch

The distance between them is clearly closing, but at the same time, there's a very human part of Chise that is growing more independent.

31 "But just this once, I want to try."

Everything Chise has experienced has led her to this moment. Her desire to help the leannán sídhe and Joel is genuine, but on top of that, she wants to involve herself in a love between human and fae and where that takes them. She has the power to act, and doesn't want to sit back and watch.

SUMMARY

Chise begins making the fairy ointment to help Joel and the leannán sídhe. At first she struggles to control the flow of her magic, but she ultimately manages to complete the ointment. When rubbed on Joel's eyes, it allows him to meet the leannán sídhe one final time. Joel thanks her and passes away.

Oberon arrives to collect the remaining ointment, but then Chise coughs up blood and collapses.

General Remarks

This incident of Chise making the fairy ointment shows both her potential as a mage and her weaknesses. We've seen her perform the purification in the Ulthar arc and have seen her making routine medicines, but this is the first time we've seen her tackle a serious magical ritual as a mage.

Without the aid of the faeries, Chise gains further understanding of what mages are.

Meanwhile, the story of the leannán sídhe and Joel comes to a close. This is the story of a love between fae and human, and points to one possible future that may await Chise and Elias.

Chapter Title

A contented mind is a perpetual feast" is an English expression originating in the biblical Book of Proverbs. If one's heart is fulfilled, it's like enjoying a banquet that never ends. If someone is satisfied, their life is one of constant happiness. The expression is sometimes worded as "a continual feast."

The Old Testament Book of Proverbs has many such sayings, and the following verse is where this one is found: "All the days of the afflicted are evil: but he that is of a merry heart hath a continual feast" (Proverbs 15:15). Japanese has several similar expressions, like "He who understands enough is always rich" or "Satisfaction is better than riches."

is made by steeping them in water, and where Chise touches it, magic is infused. This gives the cut plants fresh life and causes dramatic growth.

The lid unscrews itself without shattering the glass because the lid itself is also being influenced by the magic.

4 "Focus. Focus. Focus…"

In any magical ritual, the most critical thing is for the caster to keep their mind focused on the ritual's purpose. Since magic involves a wish powerful enough to affect the world's natural laws, the strength of that wish can have a significant effect on the result.

This involves changing not just the world but yourself, replacing the current reality with one in which your wish has been granted. To make that happen, mages undergo training to focus their minds.

Chise focuses on her magic, and the distractions around her fade away.

1 "A scent… We smell it. We smell…"

Faeries peering out between the branches. When a magical ritual sends ripples through the laws of nature, they detect that magic as a scent. The timeframe may be a little off, but magic often goes outside the flow of time, even into the future.

Here, that sensation travels through the forest spirits to the faerie king, Oberon. He can read more deeply into the signs and sense the impending disturbance, and it is his duty to take action against the sleigh beggy.

2 Title Page

Chise protected by thorns in the glow of magical lights. Thorns are Elias' symbol, but these lights are coming from Chise herself.

3 Plants Pushing the Lid Off and Spilling Out of the Jar

Seasonal plants and four-leaf clovers are the primary ingredients. Fairy ointment

8 "I see it as the color of starlight..."

In the world of modern magic, it's common to compare spiritual glows to the light of the stars—a light from another world, unleashed unto ours.

The word "astral" refers to this spiritual plane, but itself has roots in the word "star." According to *Encyclopedia of Fairyology* by Kimie Imura, when comparing faeries to celestial bodies, they should be compared not to the sun and the moon but to the stars.

9 "Gather it up, weave it together, cradle it gently..."

Mental visualizations are critical for handling magic, as is not agitating the magic or sparking growth in the plants. The idea is to lull them to sleep, compelling them to relax in the waters until the medicinal effects are released.

10 The Leannán Sídhe Passing Through the Wall

5 Chise Stands in Darkness

Chise is now linked to the laws of the world.

The light rising from the jar is a portion of the magic she's applying to the medicine.

The fact that the light is headed upward is a sign that she's connected to a higher dimension, or perhaps to something like heaven.

6 "It opens my eyes to everything around me."

To see the world of magic, her Sight is heightened, allowing her to see things she normally can't.

7 "Apparently, that's actual magical energy."

Within this series, magical energy exists within living things, objects, landforms, directions, time, and concepts. It takes on all manner of hues.

Being able to perceive these allows one to directly manipulate them.

15　14　13　12　11　10

Chise's Sight led to the loss of her family and to a traumatic childhood in which she was bullied at school and by the families that took her in and terrorized by things no one else could see.

14 "I appreciate people who smile around me. It's selfish, but I want those people to stay happy and keep smiling, that's all."

By framing her desires as selfish, Chise is trying to avoid placing undue burdens on those who are kind to her. Since she has yet to escape the trauma of her past, even communicating an idea like this is stressful for her, but she's doing her best to smile through it.

15 "You humans are so foolish. And so selfish."

Sometimes insults are the greatest compliments.

This "foolish," "selfish" nature is what faeries find so appealing about humans.

Faeries have no physical bodies, only ethereal ones (like ghosts), so physical obstructions pose no hinderance.

11 "That's what it means for your kind to love someone, right?"

Any "love" that faeries have for humans is impersonal, and the nature of their kind. The legends and their nature define how they *should* be, and that comes first for any creatures out of folklore, fae or otherwise.

12 "Falling in love over and over again is as natural for you as breathing is for living creatures."

Leannán sídhe and other succubus/vampire-type creatures are unable to live without loving someone. To them, to live is to fall in love with and consume another.

At this point, understanding that nature is all Chise needs to accept it.

13 "I don't like being in pain or upset. I don't like being around people who're scary or yell a lot."

20   19   18   17   16

Scones are further explained on page 100, so please refer to that for further details.

18   Ruth, Worried

As Chise's familiar, Ruth is carefully monitoring her stability and refusing to leave her side.

19   The Plants Surrounding Chise

There aren't actually plants growing out of her bed; this is a metaphorical depiction of her magic in action. Just as Elias' magic is shown taking the shape of thorns, Chise's magic is often depicted as growing plants.

16   "Here."

Elias offers her a cookie with raisins or dried dates in it.

This close-up of Elias' hand shows us how dark his nails are, and the scale pattern on his skin. Both traits remind us that he is an inhuman monster.

17   "Scones...lots of cream..."

Scones are a baked good frequently eaten in English homes. Originally from Scotland, they're made by mixing wheat flour or oatmeal with baking powder and milk, and then baking the result. It's common to add butter, raisins, or dates as well. Scones fall somewhere between cookies and bread, and it's typical to put cream or jam on them and eat them with afternoon tea. They are said to originate from the flat-bread bannock made from unleavened barley. The word may come from Middle Dutch "schoonbrood" (fine white bread), but another possible source for the word is the Stone of Destiny in the town of Scone in Perth.

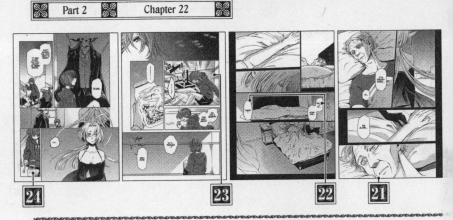

24   23   22   21

22 "Hello...? Is someone there?

Joel can't see her, but he knows there's someone by the side of his bed. Knowing that he isn't dying alone is a great help.

The leannán sídhe is not here to feed. She sits on the edge of his bed, her back to him, passing the time in his company. She feels that she shouldn't be with him, but she yearns to be. The distance between them balances her guilt and longing.

23 Chise Sleeping on the Floor

Trying to keep from falling asleep, Chise moved from the bed to the hard floor, hoping that even if she started drifting off the pain would wake her. This isn't good for you, so don't try it at home.

24 The Shell

Bivalvia shells have often been used for small amounts of ointment. Different types of clams are very good for this use.

When Elias used the transportation spell to carry them away from London in chapter 1, his magic was shown as thorns surrounding them.

20 "Something vital is draining out of me."

As the leannán sídhe drains Joel's life essence away, his body nears its limit.

Even normal old age can feel quite a bit like this.

21 His Eyes Open Wide

He may not be able to see the leannán sídhe, but when she put her hand on him, he felt something.

29　　　　**28**　　　　**27**　**26**　　　　**25**

28　Peering Out Around the Roses

She wanted to meet him in the rose garden once again.

29　"You saw me. You looked at me. That... That's why I couldn't leave you."

To a faerie, to be seen is to be controlled. Being seen by a human creates a connection. The leannán sídhe is normally the one to find and consume her lovers, and she was profoundly confused by this love that began with her being discovered. It set her on this path.

Even after everything, the leannán sídhe doesn't want to admit that Joel was her lover. If she admits it, then the guilt at having consumed him will crush her. Perhaps that is why she's pushing him away.

Their relationship echoes many things in Elias and Chise's. Elias found Chise, but Chise is the one who finds the path to change.

25　"That's your choice, not mine."

If she dabs the ointment on Joel's eyelids, he'll be able to see the leannán sídhe. It seems likely that they'll be able to speak to each other as well.

But this will violate the fae taboo and capture the leannán sídhe in a human's sight...and it will make it clear that the leannán sídhe is the one killing him. Either of these factors will bring her grief.

26　Eyelids

The fairy ointment administered to Joel's eyelids.

This erases the magical effect that prevents faeries from being seen and enables him to see them.

The leannán sídhe has chosen to reveal herself to Joel.

27　"My garden..."

Joel can no longer stand on his own, but the leannán sídhe chose the rose garden where they first met as the place to show herself to him, and moved him here.

33 "I glimpsed you for just a moment."

Here she learns that he shared her feelings.

34 "From that day on, my life wasn't empty anymore."

People can't live empty lives. Their days must have some value. This is vital to mental health.

Joel tried to fill the void in his heart by tending to the roses his wife left him, but it was the fleeting encounter with the leannán sídhe that gave it meaning.

To convey how his own heart is beating, he reaches out and touches her for the first time, placing her hand on his chest. Even knowing that his pulse is growing feeble, he wants her to understand how meeting her makes his heart soar.

30 "You said you were scared!"

The leannán sídhe admits that she was standing by his bed, and Joel recognizes the admission for what it is.

31 "A fae who blesses a man she loves with inspiration, and takes his life in return."

Everyone English, especially bookworms, knows about leannán sídhe, even if they've never seen one.

For an English book-lover compelled to toil away at his writing, even if the results are nothing special, a leannán sídhe would be a dream come true.

He held this belief strongly enough to immediately see her for what she is.

32 "You have [given]."

To be loved by someone is to receive many things, many of them intangible.

| 40 | 39 | 38 | 37 | 36 | 35 |

unintentionally consumed enough for all the time they spent together. Joel gave all of himself to her and returned to dust.

39 "You...didn't even give me time to answer."

A leannán sídhe's love is a contract. Normally one will only drain a human's life with their consent, and will give the human talent in exchange. Humans are generally unaware that this has occurred, instead believing the contract to have been a dream or hallucination, but they still must consent, even if unconsciously.

In Joel's case, their reunion and conversation were his form of consent.

40 Chise Behind the Roses

Chise helped arrange this meeting, and has watched over it from the shadows.

Knowing that to be the case, the leannán sídhe explains to Chise how it made her feel.

35 "I don't know what's waiting for me beyond the veil."

Some Christians believe that after death they will go to purgatory and await judgment, but that only a select few are allowed into heaven. The gates of heaven are quite narrow. Joel isn't sure he'll be able to see his wife again.

36 "But I think some part of me will return to be with you."

A vow for the next life—a promise that Joel's love will conquer time and the difference between their natures.

37 "So my life is yours. Please take it."

He accepts the leannán sídhe's nature and chooses to express his love by allowing her to take his life. This is a profound demonstration of love.

38 Joel Vanishes

Normally, when a faerie drains someone, the flesh remains, but the leannán sídhe

45 "I could not say. But seeing you cry makes me feel peculiar. As if something inside me is… squirming."

Elias still does not understand these feelings.

46 "I'm sorry. I'm not being a very good teacher."

Yet Chise's actions here provide an opportunity for Elias to reflect.

47 "It's weird, though. My stomach feels like it's gurgling."

Chise's body had been producing vast quantities of magic to help create the ointment, and the circuits are still engaged. Even with the ointment complete, they're going full speed ahead, and her body can't keep up with it. Until this moment, her ring was keeping the magic contained, but the ring has begun to crack.

48 "Oberon?!"

The faerie king. For more, see *Supplement I*, page 86.

41 "I'll wait here for Joel, even if he doesn't come back to me until the end of the world."

The leannán sídhe vows to overcome her nature out of love for Joel.

42 Stone Wall

To ward off the strong winter winds of England, you see many such stone walls. These often follow defensive walls built during the days of the Roman Empire.

43 "Is that 'grief'?"

Elias does not completely understand Chise's emotions. Chise, for her part, hasn't noticed her own tears.

The Ancient Magus' Bride makes liberal use of panel layouts that imitate cinematic editing tricks, using the reader's point of view to heighten the drama.

44 The Package

She's holding the jar against herself, wrapped in cloth.

Cream Tea With Scones

Scones are an essential part of afternoon tea, baked and eaten in homes across England. They're often served with jam and clotted cream. This tradition is formally known as a "cream tea." In high-class English society, the evening was often taken up by the theater or other social events, so dinner could be served as late as nine; by having a light afternoon tea earlier in the day, people didn't go hungry between meals.

This particular style of afternoon tea is said to have begun in Devonshire. It is best done by breaking a warm scone in half, spreading cream on it, and then topping it with jam.

49 "Fairy ointment, huh?"

When faerie children are born, to give them a fae's Sight, this ointment is rubbed on their eyelids.

50 "Humans making it is a giant no-no."

In the past, there were a fair number of humans who could see faeries, and many mages who made fairy ointment. But humans misused it, employing it for their own benefit, so making and using it became taboo.

In the fairytale "The Fairy Nurse," the woman who accidentally rubs some of this ointment on her eyes gains the power to see faeries, and later sees a faerie steal some butter. As punishment, she's blinded in the eye that has the Sight.

But here, all Oberon has to do is collect the remaining ointment, and the problem is resolved.

How to See Faeries

DISCUSSION 4: **Fairy Ointment and How to See Faeries**

Chise puts herself at risk to make the fairy ointment, but were there any other ways to allow Joel to see the leannán sídhe?

According to Kimie Imura's *Encyclopedia of Fairyology*, methods for seeing faeries include borrowing the power of someone who can see them (the second sight), resting a four-leaf clover on one's head, and overturning the soil on a fairy mound. It's also said that humans can see faeries at specific times of year (midsummer night's eve) or times of day (twilight).

However, when we actually tried placing a four-leaf clover on our heads, we did not gain the ability to see faeries. It seems that this isn't possible for those without an innate talent for magic. It's uncertain whether he would have been able to see even with the help of Chise's Sight.

In volume 3, page 125, it seems as if Joel is able to see the leannán sídhe, but whether that would work again as he lies dying is extremely doubtful.

Making an attempt at a certain time of day likewise offers no certainty. Joel's health is a major factor here. Turning the soil on a fairy mound is dangerous, given how time flows differently in the faeries' lands. If you knew exactly where to look, perhaps it could work, but months might pass while you searched in vain. All things considered, the only sure way to allow Joel to see faeries was to make the fairy ointment.

DISCUSSION 4: Fairy Ointment and How to See Faeries

In days of yore, it was believed that rubbing fairy ointment on your eyelids would allow you to see faeries and grant you clear sight, allowing you to see their true form.

Joseph Jacobs, an anthropologist who specialized in English folklore, collected a story called "The Fairy Nurse" in which a nurse accidentally rubbed ointment intended for a faerie baby on her own eyelid, thus gaining the ability to see their true forms. But since it's forbidden for humans to use fairy ointment, the nurse faced the wrath of the faerie king and was blinded in the affected eye.

Different sources describe the ointment as being made of crushed four-leaf clovers or as being a mix of four-leaf clover, St. John's wort, red verbena, and daisies.

In *Yousei no Sodatekata* (by Ryo Katsuragi and Minae Takada [Hakusensha]), since seeing Japanese faeries requires Japanese plants, they take water infused with kadsura bark, add seasonal flowers, and steep it in alcohol. This appears to have been a significant influence on the author.

The process of bathing the ointment in moonlight and sunlight in the four cardinal directions (as depicted in chapters 21-22) also seems to be derived from *Yousei no Sodatekata*.

Perhaps he could catch a fleeting glimpse. But it's difficult for ordinary humans to see faeries consistently.

In Celtic culture, three-leaf clovers are called shamrocks.

Four-leaf clovers are considered a sign of good luck, even in Japan.

Not to get sidetracked, but the reason the four-leaf clover is considered good luck is because it resembles the cross. The chances of a clover having four leaves is somewhere between 1/5,000 and 1/10,000, so they're quite rare indeed.

According to folklore, a two-leaf clover is a sign of faith, a three-leaf clover a sign of love, and a five-leaf clover a sign of fortune. Ireland has long called the three-leaf clover a "shamrock" and made it their national symbol.

Yousei no Sodatekata indicates that another method of meeting faeries involves taking three-leaf clovers (shamrocks), placing one on your head, and turning seven times in a place where faeries are likely to be found.

and is considered a variation on Leg Peeping. Another similar method involves holding a gun upside-down and peering down the sights, while peering through an upside-down window has long been believed to be a means of seeing into another world.

The Stone Chise Carries

Another means of peering through an opening that allows you to see the other world is the stone Chise carries, the one with a naturally-formed hole. Stones like this have many names, including witch stones, hag stones, or adder stones, and are said to have the power to dispel magic.

Such holes can form in types of rock (igneous or sedimentary) that have qualities that make holes form easily, or stones that have their weakest sections carved away by rivers and oceans. Such stones found on coasts are often stones where a shellfish has slowly bored a hole.

On the Orkney Islands in Scotland, there once stood a massive rock with a large hole in it. It was called the Odin Stone. Couples who passed through the hole were considered legally married. Unfortunately, this stone no longer exists. In 1814, the man leasing the land with the stone on it, Captain Mackay, grew sick of the number of pilgrims visiting the stones and ruining the land, and he and his men knocked the stones down. The remains were permanently destroyed in 1940.

The Fox's Window

In Japan, two methods of seeing yokai or distinguishing yokai from ordinary things are the Fox's Window (or Hole) and Leg (or Sleeve) Peeping.

Toru Tsunemitsu's *Shigusa no Minzokugaku* (Kadokawa Sophia Bunko) says that to form a Fox's Window, you place the backs of your hands together, passing the index finger of one hand through the little and ring fingers of the other, the ring and middle fingers below the other index finger, and then the thumb on top of that—quite a tangle! But peering through the gap left in the center allows you to see ghosts and tell if a person is a fox in disguise.

Tsunemitsu writes that this involves weaving the fronts and backs of the fingers of both hands together, eliminating the boundary between the surface world and the hidden one and allowing one to peer into that hidden world.

Leg Peeping involves placing the feet apart, bending over, and peering through the legs upside-down. Seeing the world from this unexpected perspective has the power to break through a yokai's deception. In 2006, Atsuki Higashiyama from Ritsumeikan University and Kohei Adachi from Osaka University proved that this method actually does alter perceptions. (This research received the Ig Nobel Prize for Perception in 2016.)

Sleeve Peeping involves peering through the gap below a kimono sleeve

Beliefs involving stones with holes also exist in Indonesia, where a ritual known as Batu Berlubang is performed.

In Japan's Okayama Prefecture, we find the Mimiou Meishin, which is believed to have the power to cure ear-related illness if one offers up a stone with a hole in it.

Since England and Japan both have beliefs involving the power of stones with holes, we can see that it's a strange connection between the far eastern and far western edges of the Eurasian continent.

SUMMARY

The process of making the fairy ointment has taken a severe toll on Chise's body. As her magic ring breaks, she coughs up blood and collapses. Oberon blames her physical frailty and takes her to the Faerie Kingdom.

Shannon, a changeling doctor, is able to keep Chise alive, but Chise's wounds refuse to close. Shannon takes drastic steps to jump-start the healing process.

Meanwhile, Titania, the faerie queen, urges Elias to remain in the Faerie Kingdom, but he refuses.

Once Chise has finally healed, she and Elias return to the surface world…where it is now winter, thanks to differences in how time flows in the two worlds.

CHAPTER **23** Fools rush in where angels fear to tread.

General Remarks

The final chapter of the fairy ointment arc. When Chise exceeds her body's limits while making the ointment, she and Elias head to the Faerie Kingdom. Chise meets the changeling doctor Shannon, and learns how important it is to actively want to live. For his part, Elias admits that he values Chise's humanity. Both revelations point to the bond between them.

This chapter cuts back and forth between the conversation between Chise and Shannon and the one between Elias and Titania, deepening the significance of each discussion.

Chapter Title

Fools rush in where angels fear to tread" is from a poem by Alexander Pope (1688-1744), *An Essay on Criticism*.

Those with little experience or knowledge are unaware of their own inadequacies, and throw themselves into things with no thought for the consequences. The wise think things through, and act carefully. The expression is a warning against the danger of acting on impulse.

Pope continues, "But rattling nonsense in full volleys breaks;

　And never shock'd, and never turn'd aside,

　　Bursts out, resistless, with a thund'ring tide."

Elias' actions in this chapter don't directly reflect the meaning of this expression, but with Chise's magic out of control, he is forced to take refuge in the Faerie Kingdom to save her.

4 "Get back into her shadow, will you?"

Fae normally exist without physical bodies, and manifesting this way only strengthens the sympathetic connection Ruth has with Chise. By temporarily abandoning his physical form and retreating to her shadow, Ruth can reduce the damage to himself for the time being.

5 "This is no time to take root, Thorn's Child!"

Another name for Elias, the Thorn Mage. Mostly used by high-level fae like Oberon and Titania.

6 "Time flows too quickly here."

Time in the real world flows fast, and Chise has little time left. If they go to the other side (the Faerie Kingdom), they can minimize the ravages of time.

7 "It's not as if a human doctor could treat her for this."

It would be difficult for a human doctor

1 Title Page

Chise balling herself up underwater. Light is streaming down from above her, but she is oblivious to it.

Sinking to the bottom of a body of water is a metaphor for the depths of the mind. If she can find something down here and bring it back to the surface with her, she'll be able to take steps to change her situation.

2 "Looks like her ring wasn't up to the job."

The ring was suppressing her generation of magic.

3 "A binding with a mortal always drags us closer to them than the reverse."

As Chise's familiar, Ruth's life is bound to hers, and he suffers sympathetic damage when she's injured. If Chise dies, Ruth will die with her.

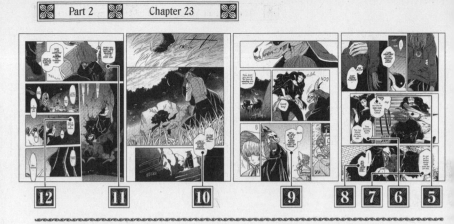

See chapter 1. Chise was tricked by an ariel who attempted to bring her through this entrance to the Faerie Kingdom.

In chapter 1, the ariel invites Chise to the Faerie Kingdom, but Chise declines.

12 "But it brings a robin."

The Japanese here is the kanji for "honey mead" with the English word "robin" in the furigana. Honey mead was often used in ancient times as an offering to gods and spirits, and fae are drawn to it, as they are to sleigh beggy. Calling it (and a sleigh beggy) "robin" is poetic license on the part of the author.

to understand Chise's condition, or for Elias to explain it. The chances of a human doctor being able to heal her are extremely low, and if Chise were hospitalized, it could lead to difficult legal repercussions.

8 "No, but the faerie kingdom..."

Elias has long been reluctant to dwell there.

9 "Silky. We'll be away for a time. Please watch over the house."

As a house spirit, Silky will protect the home without being told. But Elias is making this request as family.

10 "In the heart of this hill lies a doorway to the faerie kingdom."

The Tuatha Dé Danann went beneath a hill and became small gods. In Ireland and Celtic cultural areas, there are many ancient stone-based cultural ruins said to be linked to the Faerie Kingdom.

11 "When you came here before, I reached out to stop you."

people believed emotions resided in the heart, so it was viewed as an important organ, magically speaking. But the idea that magic flows through the body like blood bears a closer resemblance to ancient Greek beliefs in humorism (the belief that the body contained four humors, and that the balance controlled your well-being), Chinese Wu Xing (Five Elements), or other holistic beliefs (which look at the body as a whole rather than the functions of individual parts).

16 "You generated way too much magical energy, and the strain made your body start to rupture."

Even in the real world, major shocks—such as machine gun bullets striking the limbs—can send shockwaves through the blood vessels, causing ruptures in the heart and brain that lead to death.

17 Shannon

A name that originated in Ireland, which is widely used as either a last name or a

13 "You will *not* touch her."

Sleigh beggy like Chise unconsciously produce magic whenever faeries touch them. In her current condition, even the blood dripping from her is as sweet as honey mead to the faeries, but that won't help her.

Elias is displeased at being forced to return to the Faerie Kingdom like this, and his temper is rather frayed.

14 Chise Covered in Bandages.

Chise's eyes are covered with bandages because magic easily collects in the eyes, and there's a real risk of it causing ruptures there. For her own safety, she has been temporarily prevented from seeing. Chise's Sight is particularly strong, so her eyes need to be cared for.

15 "Magic flows through your veins like blood. Your internal organs are saturated with it."

This concept is original to *The Ancient Magus' Bride*. In older times in Europe,

In many cases, a newborn will be switched with a faerie baby, but they could also be replaced with wooden rods or stocks (wooden dolls), wrinkly old people, faeries that can no longer move, or strange, ugly babies.

According to Kimie Imura's *Encyclopedia of Fairyology*, changelings can be identified in a number of ways, including throwing them into boiling water, applying hot pokers, or showing them unusual things. For instance, one bar hostess given a changeling pretended to brew alcohol in 20 eggshells, and as she was lining the shells up by the fire the baby suddenly said, "I've lived 800 years and never seen anyone brew alcohol like that!" revealing that he was, indeed, a changeling.

In Shakespeare's *A Midsummer Night's Dream*, Oberon and Titania are engaged in a quarrel over a particularly adorable changeling.

19 Titania, the Faerie Queen

Oberon's wife, and ruler of the faeries. For more, see *Supplement I*, page 103.

given name for either boys or girls in all English-speaking countries. The name is derived from the River Shannon in Ireland, and there are a number of variants, like Sionainn or Shanna. The River Shannon divides Ireland into east and west, and has played a vital historical role geographically, militarily, and economically. The goddess Sionna is the granddaughter of the god of the sea, Ler (father of Manannán mac Lir). Sionna approached the forbidden well of Connla (the well of knowledge), caught and ate the salmon of wisdom, and gained great magical power. This story closely resembles myths about Fionn mac Cumhaill.

18 "I'm a changeling."

Faeries have been known to want a human baby, which leads them to exchange something for a newborn. Their reasons range from seeing human babies as cuter (as seen in Shakespeare's *A Midsummer Night's Dream*) to simple mischief or to getting rid of a faerie that has grown old and immobile.

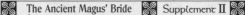

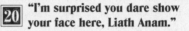

the natures change. For more, see the next chapter (24) or "The War at the Walshes'" in *The Silver Yarn* anthology novel.

23 "I trust you've made sure your feelings are mutual?"

When a relationship isn't working out, most of the time it comes down to a lack of communication.

Shannon had a lot of problems when she first started living with Shanahan, and is worried that this young girl is going through something similar.

24 Shanahan

Shanahan is a surname found in many English-speaking counties. The name originally comes from Ireland, and it's related to "Shannon."

This Shanahan is like a centaur, in that the lower half of his body has four legs like either a lion or a wolf. This arguably makes him an androsphinx (or male sphinx), but it seems likely we should simply consider him a variant on creatures found within Celtic bestiaries.

20 "I'm surprised you dare show your face here, Liath Anam."

This seems to imply that Elias brought misfortune to the faerie world at some point in the past, but as yet, details have not been revealed.

The faerie guardian at Titania's side, Spriggan, is the protector of the fae, and is prone to this sort of hostile behavior to anyone on the human side.

21 The Ant

Chise is being carried by a faerie ant (a muryan). Muryans once had human forms, and even after becoming ants, they often continue to wear human clothing.

22 "Some types of fae experience illness and age, like humans and beasts."

Not all faeries are immortal. Whether they're caught up in some real-world mess that leads to them aging or to the deterioration of the environment they preside over, their health can collapse or

Humans tend to reject people who don't fit within their ideas of normalcy. Instead, such outliers are seen as a threat.

"But one night, Shanahan came to get me."

When changelings grow up unhindered, the one on the faerie side is told the truth of what they are, but the one on the human side is often unaware and troubled. There are cases where the faerie side comes to take them back.

For more on this, see Yuu Godai's story "Jack the Flash and the Rainbow Egg," carried in two parts in the novel anthologies *The Golden Yarn* and *The Silver Yarn*.

"Humans get scared and suspicious when someone doesn't age normally."

Compared to humans, faeries barely age. One wouldn't show signs of growing older in a mere fifty years. But for a human, that's unnatural.

"I'm making tsukiyotake mushroom soup for dinner!"

Tsukiyotake ("moon night mushroom") is a mushroom of the Agaricales order, found growing on beech trees in late summer and fall. It is bioluminescent and glows in the dark, so it is also called yami-yotake ("dark night mushroom"). It contains the poison Illudin S, and consuming it leads to diarrhea and vomiting or even death. Making it into a soup would not eliminate the poison, so don't try it.

"Any human who stays in the faerie kingdom for long becomes something different."

Magic is part of the environment. Spending time with faeries and soaking in their magic turns you into something neither fae nor human. Once that happens, one does not fully belong to either world, but can end up fae enough to not be rejected by other faeries.

"I was a doctor at the local hospital. Most of my peers weren't fond of me."

34 **"The mortal realm is poison to the heart."**

To fae or sleigh beggy (who are quite like fae), the friction and stress of the human world and the unpleasantness of human emotions all act like poison. It corrupts them, and contact with it dulls the purity of the fae.

35 **"You'd serve her best by helping her shed her human trappings."**

This serves to emphasize the story we just heard about Shannon and Shanahan.

They both shed their human trappings and are now living contently in the Faerie Kingdom. But to do so may involve abandoning the human form, as in Shanahan's case.

36 **"She'll almost certainly die far too young."**

Chise's fragility will be the death of her. But if she becomes fae and sheds her human form, she may be able to surpass that limitation.

30 **"I lived my life and did my job to the best of my ability. I have nothing to be ashamed of."**

Shannon takes pride in her work as a doctor. She resents being rejected because of her origins.

31 **"A lake…?"**

Clear lakes harbor spiritual energy and healing power. In Ireland, lakes like this are called lough and are said to be the domain of the giant goddess who made the land.

32 **As a fae, I can't help being drawn to a sleigh beggy."**

This is clearly a trait common among all types of fae.

33 **"But I find that I detest you."**

Shannon finds herself trapped between two contradictory impulses—her nature as a fae and her human-trained scientific mind. Here she follows her faerie nature and acts accordingly.

10 **"It's true that humans fear me, but they are also the ones who have accepted me for who and what I am."**

Humans fear things that are different, and they see Elias as a monster. On the other hand, that fear doesn't last for long. Over time, some have grown to accept Elias.

While the faerie world never changes, the human world is one of possibility.

11 **"That is why…" "Eyes forward. Not on the ground."**

These lines aren't actually connected, but they're linked by virtue of being drawn on the same page. As Elias' feelings for humans surface, they reach Chise's heart while she drowns. These words from way back in chapter 1 are recalled and given new meaning. Shannon's arms become the collar and chains.

37 **"Titania…I…"**

As Elias hesitates, we see Chise drowning in the lake. Their mental states are in sync here.

38 **"You fae eternally look down on me in one way or another."**

Like Chise, Elias is rejected by his own kind, scorned as a half-thing and a foul creature. Since fae are immortal, that attitude is not going to change no matter how many centuries pass.

39 **A Vision While Drowning**

As Shannon holds Chise under the water and Chise begins to drown, Shannon's grip reminds Chise of the time her mother nearly strangled her—the trauma she needs to overcome.

such a shock that Chise wasn't even capable of resisting.

Her mother ultimately let her go and chose to take her own life instead, and Chise has lived with that curse ever since. But now, at last, the will to resist manifests within her.

45 "Sometimes, the most powerful force a living creature can draw on is their will."

Just as magic in this world borrows power to impose your desires on the natural laws, a creature's own will can mean the difference between life and death.

Especially here in the Faerie Kingdom, where magic is a powerful force, willpower alone determines who survives.

46 "That's why your wounds didn't close."

Without the will to heal and live, even the magic of the Faerie Kingdom couldn't help her recover.

42 "Keep your chin up, and your spine straight. Understood?"

Words Elias said back in chapter 1, right after purchasing Chise. Elias is not physically present with her now, but in this moment he seems to stand before her.

The page's layout provides a dramatic presentation.

43 "Given the choice, I wish for Chise to live her life as a human."

Elias may be considered a monster, but through Chise, he has met humans.

While both Elias and Titania tend to refer to Chise as a child, the kanji Elias uses is for human children and the one Titania uses is for young animals.

44 Chise Resists Shannon

The day her mother strangled her, Chise was unable to fight back. Her mother was much stronger, but when Chise saw her mother crying while strangling her was

one they reached from the entrance near Elias' home is called the Ant Hill. In the Danann myths, the Faerie Kingdom lies beneath a hill, and here Oberon leads Elias and Chise down a staircase. This region is called the Ant Hill because so many Muryans live here.

Muryans are a type of little people from Cornwall, referring to ant people or faerie ants. Muryan is also just the Cornish word for "ant." They're generally said to be rather small faeries, between 10 and 20 centimeters, with the ability to transform into ants. They're also said to be the souls of heretics who became faeries—unable to reach heaven due to their heresy but too pure of soul to be sent to hell, and thus given the form of ants.

On occasion they're also said to turn into birds, growing smaller each time until they become too small to see and vanish completely. By the same logic, the Tuatha Dé Danann gods grew smaller and became the faeries under the hills.

47 "She sure loves her job."

Since she was a faerie changeling, Shannon was unable to continue her life's work as a doctor in the surface world, but her pride is such that she continues being a doctor even in the Faerie Kingdom.

She provides a number of medicines that can support Chise's recovery and improve her odds of surviving. Since Shannon can't give her a transfusion, Chise especially needs the medicine that helps her generate new blood.

48 "Um, Elias? I can walk now."

On their way home, Elias carries Chise. This is what always happens, but Chise wants to return on her own two feet.

Elias, however, still wants to protect her.

Faerie Kingdom: The Ant Hill

In *The Ancient Magus' Bride* there are many regions to the Faerie Kingdom. The

he becomes a white-haired old man and finds that 300 years have passed.

There are also dreamlike tales of spending days lost in the pleasures of the faerie realm only to find that mere moments have passed in the real world.

On Magical Healing

In *The Ancient Magus' Bride* there are not many depictions of magical healing. Lindel's healing hands are effective on minor scratches but could never have healed Chise in the condition she was just in. The medicine Elias makes is effective, but it merely aids patients on their road to recovery. He has not been able to cure the root cause of Simon's respiratory condition and was unable to extend Joel's life.

When the cause is clear and the patient a pure human, medical care and nursing are best provided by real-world hospitals.

 "I even identified the emotion successfully. But you still live. That is what matters."

Elias can only describe the emotion as "shocked," but he is still able to accept Chise's actions.

"Time flows differently between the worlds, so there will be... slips."

The flow of time is different in the human and faerie realms. It might be faster or slower, but it doesn't align.

There are many stories in which time flows more slowly in the faerie realms. Someone visits their lands, stays only three days, and come back to find a hundred years have passed in the real world. Stories like the Japanese Urashima Tarou or the western Rip Van Winkle are well-known, and Celtic mythology also has a story in which Niamh's white horse takes Oisín to Tír na nÓg, where the moment Oisín slips from the horse and his foot touches the ground in the mortal realm,

116

SUMMARY

While Elias is off in the Faerie Kingdom so that Chise can be healed, Silky is left protecting the home.

Silky does the housework, tidies up, and deep-cleans the house, but when autumn comes and Elias and Chise still haven't returned, she reflects on the past.

Silky was once a banshee, but when the family she haunted died out, she was unable to fulfill her function. As she wandered, the Spriggan suggested that she protect a new home, and she transformed into a type of house spirit, a Silky (or Silkie).

As winter arrives, Chise and Elias return, reunited with their home and the waiting faerie.

CHAPTER **24**

There's no place like home.

General Remarks

This chapter is focused on Silky, the Silver Lady, who is left home alone until winter arrives while Chise and Elias are in the Faerie Kingdom.

This is a story about Silky's past, which also explains why she so rarely speaks.

Silky is a type of faerie bound to a house, so this episode connects strongly to the series keywords—"home" and "family."

We also learn about the relationship between Silky and the Spriggan, making for quite a heartwarming tale.

Chapter Title

"There's no place like home" is an expression widely used in English-speaking countries.

It's also a line in the song "Home, Sweet Home" from the opera *Clari, or the Maid of Milan* by the American playwright John Howard Payne (1791-1852). The song is well known in Japan as "Hanyuu no Yado" ("My Humble Cottage"). "'Mid pleasures and palaces/Though I may roam/Be it ever so humble/There's no place like home."

5

4

3

2

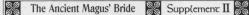
1

of water, and the other holds cleaning products and rags. The bottles are likely filled with old-fashioned cleaning supplies, which are easier for faeries to use—vinegar and oils in place of wax.

6 An Empty Speech Balloon

With no one else home, Silky decides to scrub everything.

This is a stylized manga effect that shows her enthusiasm. If you tried to letter it with appropriate sounds, it would only say something like "Mm!" or "Hmm!" rather than actual words.

An aethonic—a magical creature from the salamander family—can be seen in the corner.

7 Duster

When cleaning, it's best to start up high and work your way down, which helps keep dust from re-accumulating. Silky is using a simple duster made by placing a cloth on the end of a pole, but other types of dusters use finely cut cloth or feathers to dislodge the gathering dust.

1 Silky Left to Watch Over the House

This moment happened at the start of chapter 23, when it was still early summer.

Silky is a house faerie, so it's natural for her to be left in charge. But a home is made by people living in it, so she's alarmed to hear Elias say, "We'll be away for a time."

2 Title Page

Silky when she was a banshee, wandering through the dark forest.

3 Falling Leaves

The season is turning from summer to autumn. Chise and Elias have yet to return, and if Chise is gone, Ruth is too.

4 Wiping Dishes

There's no one home to eat meals, so the dishes remain spotless.

5 Cleaning Supplies in a Bucket

Having finished washing all the dishes in the kitchen, Silky embarks on a deep clean of the rest of the house. One bucket is full

House Faerie

Faeries of this type live in and watch over specific houses. In a broader sense, the term includes gods or spirits that protect homes, even yokai like the zashiki-warashi.

House faeries that help with housework, like brownies, are also called domestic faeries, and they offer their assistance in exchange for the simple reward of a cup of milk placed somewhere warm, like over the fireplace. The brownies from Scotland are the most famous, but there are similar spirits the world over, including the Hawaiian Menehune, the Spanish Duende, and the German Heinzelmännchen. Such spirits often grow fond of humans and are kind to them, but if promises are broken, they become angry, and if over-rewarded, they may grow satisfied and leave the house.

See *Supplement I*, page 26.

8　Mop

Floors are cleaned using cloth that absorbs water easily. (Some mops use fabric and others use bundled strings.) One wets the floor and scrubs it to get the dirt off. To keep the floor from being absolutely soaked, it's common to use a bucket with a squeezer attached, to wring excess water out of the mop.

9　Doorbell

Bells at the top of the door alert residents when company arrives. In this case, Silky's simply hung bells from a hook, but other types of doorbells employ more pliable parts to enhance the bell's swing. These are also known as chimes.

10　Whispering to the Wall Spirits

The house itself harbors spirits, and if Silky whispers to them, they'll help with her work. Here, she whispers to the wall spirits, who help her remodel and change the house's interior layout.

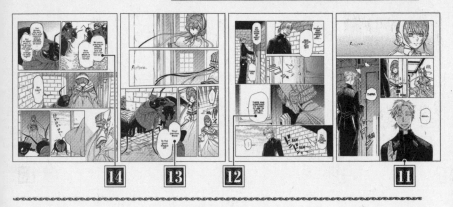

change forms they grow smaller. Being unable to switch out of ant form is a sign of maturation.

Sadly, Silky is no mage, and has no way of helping them.

15 "Sweets!!"

It's nearly Hallowe'en and there are children on her doorstep, so Silky gives them sweets. This scene is a play on the concept of "trick or treat."

One of the best-known symbols of modern Hallowe'en is the Jack-o'-lantern, made by carving a face into a hollowed-out pumpkin.

11 Simon

Simon Cullum is the priest assigned to watch Elias. Silky is not a fan.

12 "There was something I'd hoped to ask of him, but, ah well."

Simon suffers from a chronic respiratory condition, and frequently treats the symptoms with Elias' medicine. He can make do with over-the-counter medicines, but the side effects of Elias' concoction are less harsh.

Silky is well aware of this, and isn't totally unsympathetic, but as she can't speak, she answers by knocking.

13 "Your pardon, Miss!"

A pair of the Muryan ant faeries from chapter 23.

14 "We were playing at shape-shifting and we did it for too long. Now we're stuck in our ant forms!"

Muryan have human forms and can become ants or birds, but each time they

a bonfire and offer sacrifices, praying for prosperity and peace. People would take portions of this fire home to light their fireplaces and keep evil spirits at bay. They would also wear masks (to hide themselves from spirits) and dance.

November 2nd was called the Feast of All Souls, and people would offer prayers for the dead trapped in purgatory. They would wear masks to get a sweet known as a soul cake, and comfort the dead. This was known as Souling, and eventually evolved into the modern day practice of children going door to door, begging for candy by saying, "Trick or treat."

Hallowe'en (from All Hallows' Eve or All Saints' Eve) is not originally a Christian festival, but an old Celtic one (Samhain, held at the start of winter) adapted to the needs of Christianity.

16 Silky's Dream

Silky was once alone in a wind like this.

17 Crumbled Walls

Uninhabited houses soon fall to pieces.

Hallowe'en

Hallowe'en is a Christian festival held on the night of October 31st. November 1st was a major Catholic celebration called All Saints' Day or All Hallows' Day; the night before, All Hallows' Eve, became Hallowe'en.

This was originally a Celtic celebration. According to the Celtic calendar, November 1st was the start of winter, marked with a festival called Samhain. The night before, the druids would light

as having long flowing hair, wearing gray cloaks over green dresses, and having eyes red from crying. They wear mourning robes, hide their faces beneath veils, and are found curled up beneath trees.

Hearing their voices is a sign that someone will die. Some stories say that a carriage drawn by headless black horses will arrive, carrying the coffin.

19 "The family she was haunting must have died out."

In this series, a banshee watches over a particular family and weeps for the dead on their behalf.

The faeries speaking to her are both leannán sídhe.

20 "What does that matter?"

What matters to a leannán sídhe is not physical appearance but talent. Here, they speak of poets who write with "the delicacy of a spring rainfall" and novelists "whose words are as warm and bright as sunshine."

18 "Aren't you a banshee...?"

Banshees are a type of faerie hailing from Ireland and Scotland, said to herald death. "Banshee" stems from the Gaelic for "faerie woman," and in the Scottish highlands you find stories of banshees seducing and marrying men.

Generally speaking, the banshee is a harbinger of death. They wash the robes of the dead in the river, crying out in sorrow for the next to die. For that reason, they might be called the "Bean nighe," or "little washerwomen."

Some stories claim banshees are born from the ghosts of women who die in childbirth. In these accounts, the robes they wash are stained with their own blood. If you suckle from one's withered breasts, she'll grant you three wishes.

Some regions merge the banshee and the leannán sídhe, saying that banshee grant poets talent, but in return, the poet dies young.

Irish banshees take the form of women who have died young, and are described

24　Silky Can't Cry

Having lost the family she once haunted, the banshee who will become Silky questions whether she should grieve for others. She finds that the wails won't come out.

25　The Hounds of Night

Faeries sometimes keep magic hounds to protect their fairy mounds. These hounds are called "cúsídhe" or "Cŵn Annwn." Like Black Dogs, they are large black canines. The name "Cŵn Annwn" (from Welsh folklore) means "the hounds of Annwn," where Annwn is the mythological otherworld. They're ordinarily invisible, but white hounds with red eyes are said to carry the souls of the dead to the next world; when they have no prey, it's said that they will carry off unbaptized babies or the unrepentant.

There are similar legends about devils with packs of hounds racing about the night skies and collecting human souls. These are referred to as the Wild Hunt, Dando and His Dogs, or Gabriel's Hounds.

21　The Lights of Town

She heads toward the lights, searching for a new family to watch over.

22　"If you keep it up, the family banshee will mistake you for her kind and snatch you away."

A mother scolds a crying child.

As with many stories of yokai, many fairytales came into existence to warn children against misbehavior.

The banshees watch the child being scolded. One is already haunting this family, and here she's met the banshee who will become Silky. They both hear the mother's words and smile.

23　"They say a chorus of banshees will come together to mark the passing of someone like him."

Shedding tears and weeping for the dead is their job. When a good man or a monk of great virtue dies, a number of banshee will arrive to mourn him.

 "All…I…wanted…was to…be with…them…"

The one time Silky ever speaks in this series. Her one wish.

 "Those who live there keep faithfully to the old ways."

They may be Christian, but they are still Celts. They know how to treat faeries and value these old beliefs.

 "Bloodlines will always falter."

This is how the banshee lost her place. But if she haunts a house instead, perhaps she can avoid the same fate befalling her again.

 "If the light that once warmed you has faded, perhaps it is now your turn to guard the light that shines for others."

Become a spirit that protects the house rather than a banshee that laments death.

 Spriggan

Leading these faerie hounds is a Spriggan, guardian of the fairy mound.

Spriggan are a notoriously hideous, terrifying type of faerie from Cornwall. Ghosts of giants killed by Britons past, they are small in stature but able to make themselves appear enormous. They turn up around stone circles and standing stones said to have been erected by giants, protecting the treasures hidden there. Spriggan legends suggest they are prone to thieving, but if you wear your underwear inside out, you can thwart their efforts.

In this series, the Spriggan works for Titania, the faerie queen, protecting the hill in which the faerie dwell. His name is sometimes given the kanji for "guardian."

"What's befallen your home?"

The Spriggan immediately recognizes her as a banshee, and knows how odd it is for her to be wandering the fields, far from any home.

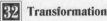

35 | "We hill folk are called to protect those in need."

"Hill folk" refers to all the faeries, the "little gods" of the Tuatha Dé Danann. In the Japanese, Spriggan mentioned protecting all the "little folk," and you might well ask, is he himself not little? But Spriggans are born from the ghosts of giants, so to his mind, he is both large and an elder.

36 | "Be well, banshee. No… Silky."

By changing the way he addresses her, he grants her a new name. Having her name used by the Spriggan gives her strength.

37 | JINGLE JANGLE

The doorbell answers her wish.

32 | Transformation

If a faerie's nature changes, they become something else. She's released from the trappings of a banshee, becoming the house spirit we know as Silky. This transformation into a housemaid's garb signifies the change in her nature.

33 | "The very picture of a silver flower in bloom."

This is why Silky is called the Silver Lady.

34 | "This suits you far better than fading away like a ghost."

A faerie who has lost their purpose, lost what defines them, is doomed to fade away, just as the heroine of "The Little Mermaid" dissolves into sea foam when her love is lost.

traced back to Old Norse or German "Alfe." Though this word means "white," it was also used in reference to a type of faerie or demon, including little folk and dream spirits. Germanic myths have stories about little folk living underground, known as "Dvergr," but these are simply a type of elf.

The concept of elves was reworked by J.R.R. Tolkien for *The Lord of the Rings*, becoming the type we see so often in modern games.

"Sídhe" means "people of the mounds." When the Tuatha Dé Danann lost to the Milesians (who became humans) they hid beneath the land and beyond the seas, diminishing in size.

Celtic fairytales came to Japan in the Meiji period, but the word "faerie" was not consistently translated as "yousei" until early Taisei. Works from the Meiji era translated it as anything from Kouda Rohan's "senjo" to Ryonosuke Akutagawa's "shouryou." "Yousei" was popularized by the early faerie translators Mineko Matsumura and Konosuke Hinatsu.

38 **"Just a moment. I'll lay a fire in the hearth."**

With Chise and Elias' return, the house is filled with sound. Faeries can't sense the cold, so Silky never lit a fire, and the place is very chilly. Chise was dressed for summer when she left, so she's half frozen.

39 **"Humans call me 'Silky.' It is my duty to nurture the light that shines within my home."**

The one time we see Silky's narration. She, too, is a woman who values the home.

Words Meaning "Faerie"

Words used for faeries have changed with the times. Generally speaking, people have used the romance-language based "fairy" or "faerie," the Germanic "elf," and the Gaelic "sídhe." "Faerie" actually comes from the French word for magic, "fay," which in turn is derived from the Latin for fortune, "fatum." "Elf" can be

SUMMARY

Home from the Faerie Kingdom, Chise and Elias settle back into their daily lives, but it's now winter and Yule is approaching. To begin preparing for Yule, they head into the forest to find a Yule log and decorations.

While they're gathering mistletoe, a Dark Lady passes by on a Horned God. Chise and Elias manage to avoid the old gods' attention and return home unscathed, where they place the Yule decorations on the door, and kiss beneath the mistletoe.

CHAPTER **25** Even the longest night has an end.

General Remarks

The period from Christmas to New Year's Day is Yule, the Celtic festival of the new year. For more on Yule, see Discussion 5: Yule and Christmas (page 159). Chapters 25-29 are a story set during Yule. This is the prologue to that storyline, and largely about the importance of Yule itself.

And at last, our main pair does something couples do.

Chapter Title

"Even the longest night has an end" is an English expression, meaning that no matter how long something unpleasant continues, there will always be an end to it. Whatever you're suffering will eventually stop. The saying is derived from a phrase in *Confessio Amantis* by the English poet John Gower (1330?-1408).

A similar phrase is found in Shakespeare's *Julius Caesar*, Act 5, Scene 1, where Brutus says, "But it sufficeth that the day will end." Shakespeare was known for this sort of dry humor. *Macbeth* contains a similar sentiment: "Time and the hour run through the roughest day."

In the context of this chapter, the saying may also refer to everything that must be done to make ready for Yule.

Chapter 25: Even the longest night has an end.

This song about the Winter Solstice, the shortest day of the year, is a creation of this series.

The singers are seasonal faeries known as the Heralds of Yule. Each has one bird-like wing, and they fly out to offer warnings about the winter solstice. They are called the messengers of the gods, but their real identity is unknown. In this series, they take the form of a girl and a boy who warn of Yule's coming.

This series draws heavily on European folklore. According to the special leaflet included in volume 7 (*Merkmal*, page 191), in Europe the robin and the wren are frequently paired together, so this design is based on that.

Norse mythology mentions a two-headed magic goat, the Yule Goat, which arrives to check if Yule preparations are complete. This was the goat that drew Thor's chariot, but it was slaughtered for a feast the gods held. After it was later revived, it became a magical beast that warned of Yule's coming.

Today, people make giant goats out of straw and wood and set them afire. Other

1 Chise Steps Outside In Boots

It is winter and the ground is covered in snow. Fully recovered now, Chise leaves her room wearing boots (ones designed to prevent slipping).

2 Title Page

The exterior of the Ainsworth home. You can see the conservatory out back. See the *Official Guide Book Merkmal*, page 62.

3 Chicken Coop

They keep chickens, allowing them to eat fresh eggs and chicken. It's likely Chise's job to feed the chickens and collect the eggs.

4 "Even at this time of day, it looks like it's just past dawn."

England's longitude is quite high. Even in the areas around London, the sun rises as late as it does in Hokkaido. Because of that, in winter, day breaks at a rather late hour.

5 "The shortest day, when the sun sleeps! The longest night, when the moon and stars rule!"

9   **8**   **7**   **6**   **5**

7 "Set the Yule Log ablaze in your hearth."

See page 135. The log of the winter solstice.

8 "Before the Horned God and his Dark Lady walk the earth."

More details can be found on page 134, but this is an old manifestation of divine figures found in Germanic myths. The "Dark Lady" is a goddess with three aspects, who may in time have been split into Frigg and Freyja. The "Horned God" refers to the antlered divine beast she rides. They are considered the precursor to the Wild Hunt.

9 "It is both the end and the beginning of the year's turning."

Since the days grow longer after the winter solstice, it marks the start of the sun's return.

January 1st is now accepted as the beginning of the new year, but that too shows the influence of the solstice.

variations have it taking human form, wandering the town like the Namahage in Japanese mythology. It may be one point of origin for Santa Claus.

6 "Hustle! Bustle! Be sure all is in order! Yuletide is upon you!"

Yule is a European winter festival that predates the arrival of Christianity. It lasts twelve days, from December 25th to January 6th. Today it incorporates Christmas, but it was originally a Viking winter festival, and even today, in Scandinavia Christmas is referred to as Yule.

The winter solstice has the fewest hours of sunlight of any day in the year, and from that day onward, the days increase in length. Thanks to that, many ancient religions marked it as the start of the new year. As a result, the European solar calendar places the New Year a week after the winter solstice festival.

Many religious rituals occur on the day Yule begins, so things can get busy. These are "offerings." Once all are complete, the Yule night begins.

example: with its green leaves and red berries all winter long, it has become a symbol of eternity and power, as well as a ward against evil, in both east and west.

But, as we see with ivy, if the same thing doesn't exist in two cultures, there's no way for similar customs to arise around it.

13 "Each land will have its own plants and powerful artifacts."

Magic is rooted in the environment and culture. What is seen as having power in that location? That's what creates the natural laws in that place; as the name implies, they are always deeply connected to the environment.

In chapter 25, Elias is finally starting to act like a magic teacher, explaining the principles of magic and background information.

14 "So that I may teach you the ways of this island country of rain and fog."

It rains nearly every day in England, so it's often referred to this way.

10 "'Samhain'?"

In the Germanic calendar, winter began on November 1st, marked by the Samhain festival. This was incorporated into Christianity, becoming Hallowe'en.

See page 121.

11 "Holly and ivy are both wards against ill fortune."

In Germanic folk tradition, bringing green leaves into the house in winter allows you to share that power of life. Furthermore, before Yule, a boy decked in holly and a girl decked in ivy paraded through the town to celebrate the arrival of the new year. This practice was incorporated into Christianity, as seen in the famous Christmas carol "The Holly and the Ivy."

12 "It stands to reason that some things are consistent from region to region."

The human race lives in harmony with nature, and this leads to similar traditions arising in different places. Holly is a good

17 16 15   14   13

grows is seen as expressing "acceptance" (pregnancy) or "lying on the bed of labor" (childbirth).

Ivy's whitish leaves are paired with the Greek goddesses Ariadne (wife of Dionysus, and goddess of revelry) and Artemis (goddess of the hunt), as well as the Celtic Arianrhod (goddess of the silver wheel).

17 "There is a proper length of time to keep them in the home."

Holly and ivy protect the home during winter, but once the New Year's festival is completely over, they must be removed from the home before Imbolc Eve (January 31st) or they'll invite misfortune.

This custom remained even after the introduction of Christianity, and the holly came to symbolize the suffering of Jesus—the thorns on the leaves represent his agony, and the red berries his blood. For that reason, all green leaves in the house must be removed before Twelfth Night.

15 "Holly's green leaves and red berries show that life continues even in the desolation of winter."

Because holly is an evergreen with distinctive red berries, it is often seen as a defense against evil. In ancient Britain, there was an earth giant named Gogmagog, peerless in prowess and vigor. He wrapped himself in holly and swung a giant club, earning him the nickname "The King of Holly." It is said that the green knight found in the Middle English text *Sir Gawain and the Green Knight* may have been Gogmagog.

16 "Ivy's shape is reminiscent of both snakes and a goddess's embrace."

The way ivy sends out flexible tendrils, wrapping them around other trees, is often linked to snakes or grapevines. Since snakes shed their skins, hibernate in winter, and can be venomous, they're often seen as signifying death and rebirth.

Holly is often seen as representing men, while ivy is seen as feminine. The way it

represent the power of nature itself. The Dark Lady is a personification of winter.

 "Oak...?"

Oak goes by many names in Japanese, and is famed for acorns, a major food source for grazing pigs in England. Forests rich in acorns have become good sources of income as a result. It's a sturdy wood, often used for ships, buildings, and furniture.

Oaks were worshipped across all of Europe, seen as trees linked to the gods. In Celtic mythology, they were the tree of the Dagda, father of the gods. The Dagda was a god of healthy appetites and lusts, and he owned a cauldron that never ran empty, providing endless food to his guests.

Oak was a magical tree devoted to the goddess of fortune, Ériu. The old name for Ireland, Éire, comes from her.

Oak was also tied to the god of thunder, and a tree used by the Celtic thunder god, Taranis, to pass along his divine will. Oak was a path leading to the land of the

"Auspicious, ancient yew is associated with both death and life, and has been revered since time immemorial."

A spirit tree called Yew by the Celts. (See page 38.) Yew symbolizes the winter solstice and is extremely long-lived, and the wood is prized because it's sturdy and long-lasting. It was often used in weapons, particularly spears and bows.

As yew trees often form hollows, they stand for both life and death. This is because yews send roots deep, connecting them to the underworld, and they were associated with the goddess Banba. In *The Book of Invasions*, she was the last queen of the Tuatha Dé Danann, and she and her two sisters, Ériu and Fódla, were great warrior queens. Yew was her tree, and known as "Banba's renown."

"Gods are to be feared and respected."

Gods in this series are magical beings with great power. They rule their domains and

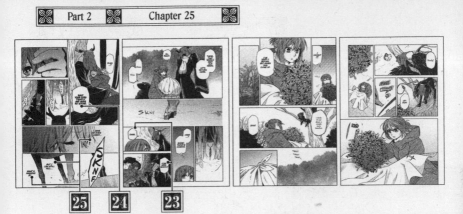

23 **"Chise. Come here. Quickly!"**

You should never stand in the path of a passing god. If you feel a god approaching, step out of their way, hide yourself, cover your eyes and ears, and protect yourself from their divine light.

24 **"Shut your eyes tightly and make no sound."**

Even a voice can be an obstruction to the god's progress, so one must remain silent in their presence.

25 **"I have my eyes closed, but I can still tell what's passing by…"**

The intensity of their presence is a particular characteristic of gods. Gods influence their surroundings just by being present. The winter goddess' very existence brings winter to her surroundings, and just encountering the horned god can end a human's life.

Someone as sensitive as Chise can't entirely tune out that presence, even with her eyes shut.

gods, and that power became stronger if mistletoe grew around it.

21 **"Mistletoe is another plant long revered for its mystic properties."**

Mistletoe is a parasitic plant of the order Santalales. They attach themselves to the bark of other trees and draw nourishment from the host, growing into rounded masses.

In Germanic and Celtic cultures, they're a holy plant, and mistletoe growing from oaks is especially prized. Frazer's *The Golden Bough* is an examination of ancient European tree-worship and describes rituals used to kill kings, but the titular Golden Bough is actually mistletoe.

22 **"Mistletoe dislikes iron and earth."**

One reason mistletoe was considered holy was that, unlike regular plants, it grows not from the ground but in the air. Therefore, its purity must not be tainted with anything earthen.

28   27   26

impregnates herself, and it passes through her belly to be reborn with new power in the spring. She dies birthing it, and is reborn as a young girl.

Triple Goddesses are found the world over. The Greek goddess Hecate—a goddess of magic who ruled over crossroads—was famed for having three faces. Selene, the moon goddess; Artemis, goddess of the hunt; and Persephone, queen of the underworld and goddess of destruction were all her in other guises. Hecate is also linked to the later goddess of love, Aphrodite.

On moonless nights, Hecate would take her hounds out to hunt—a custom similar to the Celtic Wild Hunt.

What appears here is an old god worshipped in northern Europe who grew pregnant in winter, gave birth in spring, and turned into a young girl. In Norse mythology, you can see her influence on stories about the goddess Frigg (Odin's bride, a goddess of war, magic, and prophecy) and Freyja (daughter of the sea god, Njörðr, goddess of fertility, the moon, and magic).

26 The Horned God

The Celtic hunting god Cernunnos (horned god) had antlers and hooves like a deer, and was both the ruler of the forest and a god of death who presided over the underworld.

The name "Cernunnos" is taken from letters carved into the Pillar of the Boatmen discovered in Paris.

Cernunnos was a god of fertility, deeply connected to the earth mother.

Over the years, the passage of Cernunnos and the earth mother changed into stories of the faeries and their Wild Hunt.

27 The Dark Lady

The Dark Lady is an earth mother and fertility goddess, worshipped in many locations across ancient Europe. She had three aspects, representing the phases of the moon and the changing of the seasons: a young girl, a mother (pregnant), and a crone. In anthropological contexts she's often referred to as the Triple Goddess. The version that appears here is the pregnant one. She swallows the fading sun and

[29] **"We'd best begin by setting the Yule Log alight."**

For the twelve days of Yule, it was customary to place a single log in the fireplace and keep it burning. It was considered bad luck if it went out at any point.

This practice has died out in modern times, but instead, people began to eat cakes in the shape of logs. These are also called Yule Logs, or Buche de Noel. To make them, you wrap sponge cake spread with raspberry jam and then frost the outside with chocolate, emulating the shape of a log.

[30] **"When two people stand beneath mistletoe, they're to kiss."**

Since mistletoe is associated with good fortune and fertility, kissing beneath it brings good tidings. Mistletoe is also an evergreen, a symbol of life and plenty, and a magic plant that never touches the ground, which explains the "beneath" part. If you refuse a kiss under mistletoe, it's said you will be unable to marry for the next year.

[28] **"Winter Solstice. Summer Solstice. Autumn Equinox. Spring Equinox. Everyone ventures out to mark the changing of the seasons."**

These divided the seasons in the Celtic calendar. Celtic seasons had eight major days dividing them.

Beltane (May 1st): The beginning of summer.
Midsummer (June 21st): The summer solstice.
Lughnasadh (August 1st): The peak of summer.
Mabon (September 21st): The autumn equinox.
Samhain (November 1st): The beginning of winter.
Yule (December 21st): The winter solstice.
Imbolc (February 1st): The end of the new year.
Ostara (March 21st): The spring equinox.

(From Jane Gifford's *The Celtic Wisdom of Trees: Mysteries, Magic, and Medicine.*)

35 A Bird

This bird is Alice's familiar. There are magic sigils on its eyes and forehead.

The cylinder hanging from its neck is for carrying messages.

This was once a real bird, but the eyes (easily damaged and quick to rot) have been removed, replaced with crystal balls that operate like cameras. Replacing easily damaged parts with mechanical bits and metal is a type of artificing, but not as complicated as a magus craft.

36 Alice

Apprentice and bodyguard to Renfred, the one-armed alchemist. She's better at physical things than she is at magic, so Renfred made her his bodyguard so she could remain at his side without it feeling awkward. It may be only a pretext, but that's how the two of them make things work.

In ancient Europe, trees were believed to be the root of all life, so this may have been an early form of courtship or a rite of hierogamy.

31 "I've heard of it many times, but have never done it myself."

Elias is curious, but in that sense, he does not fully grasp the significance.

32 "Looks like he really does want to try."

Chise can sense that Elias truly wants to try this custom. She's learned to read a lot of nuance from that bone head of his, and the two have been growing closer.

33 Chise hesitates

She's uncertain what part of that skull to kiss. Since he's all bone, he has no lips, and besides, Chise herself feels like it's a little early for a real kiss.

34 "And for you."

Instead of the usual forehead or temple, Elias tries going for the cheek. Cats and dogs often go for the cheek, too.

Part 3

SUMMARY

On Christmas Eve, Alice, Renfred's apprentice/bodyguard, asks Chise to go into the city. Chise slips out of the house without telling Elias, and heads to London with Ruth.

Alice is hoping for Chise's help picking out a Christmas present for Renfred. It hadn't even occurred to Chise to get something for Elias, so the two of them go out shopping.

Along the way, they meet a centaur delivering something from Elias to Angelica, and he offers some gift-buying advice. Chise gets an idea, but when Alice tries to pry it out of her they attract the attention of some drug dealers Alice used to work with. Ruth helps them get away.

Resting on the riverbank, Alice apologizes for getting Chise mixed up in that trouble, and Chise asks about Alice's past.

CHAPTER 26

God's mill grinds slow but sure. I

General Remarks

This chapter calls back to some fore-shadowing from all the way back in chapter 12. During the Black Dog arc (chapters 9-12), the alchemist Renfred's apprentice, Alice, went from being an enemy to a temporary ally. Now she and Chise are close enough to wander around London, searching for presents for their masters, and the events of this story show them growing even closer.

Chapter Title

"God's mill grinds slow but sure" is an English expression. It's also some-times written "The mills of God grind slowly." This concept comes from the Greek biographer Plutarch, and means that all sins will be judged equally in the eyes of the Lord. It's similar to the Japanese expression that means "Heaven's net has large meshes, but nothing escapes."

In this chapter, Alice discovers that the sins of her past have come back to haunt her, and Elias is monitoring Chise's (modest) scheme.

One for sorrow,
Two for mirth,
Three for a funeral,
And four for birth.

As we'll later learn, this particular magpie is Alice's familiar. There's a message holder hanging from its neck.

3 Title Page

A Christmas tree, since chapters 26 and 27 revolve around the holiday.

Evergreen branches and leaves were thought to be a defense against evil, and decorating the home with them was a custom not only in Europe but in Egypt and China. The custom of decorating Christmas trees appears to have originated in Germany between the 15th and 16th centuries. In England, the practice spread after Queen Victoria decorated a tree for her German husband, Prince Albert, in 1840.

1 SNIP SNIP SNIP

Elias is up late, cutting fabric. When he needs to infuse something with magic, he may wear his robes to work, but in this case...well, what he's doing will be revealed in chapter 27.

2 "A magpie...?"

A bird of the Passeriformes order, Corvidae family. Magpies are primarily found on the Eurasian continent, and there are many subspecies. In English, the Eurasian magpie is just one of many birds referred to as magpies.

Due to their reputation for picking up anything shiny, the word "magpie" often has connotations of thievery. The English/Irish nursery rhyme "One for Sorrow" describes how the number of magpies you see may tell the future. Below is the version collected in 1780 by the English antiquarian John Brand.

7 Train

The standard 3+2 seat layout seen in many commuter trains around London. Judging by the layout, this model is likely a Networker, either a Class 165 or 166. Famed for their cramped interiors.

8 Marble Arch

The Marble Arch was modeled on the Arch of Constantine in Rome.

The meeting spot Chise heads to is the Marble Arch, which stands at the entrance to Hyde Park, one of four Royal

4 "For some reason, I don't feel like I should tell him directly..."

Chise sneaks out without telling Elias where she's going, but Elias is fully aware.

5 "That trinket Angelica gave me is in here somewhere..."

Elias is rummaging for a tracking device— a magus craft he had made. More of a drone than a familiar, it appears to have tiny eyes. It flies after its target, tracking and monitoring them.

6 Train Station

This station is believed to be modeled on Moreton-in-Marsh to the north of the Cotswolds. Assuming Chise did board the Great Western Railway here, she would have to transfer at Paddington to the London Underground's District line, or at Notting Hill Gate to the Central line, and head from there to the Marble Arch tube station.

12   "We can chat over a bite to eat."

The menu includes shepherd's pie, fish and chips, fried chicken and baked beans, bangers and mash, and scotch eggs—a parade of famous English foods. Both girls are voracious eaters.

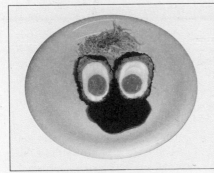

Scotch eggs are hardboiled eggs wrapped in ground meat and deep-fried. Commonly eaten cold.

Parks in London. As the name implies, it's made of marble. It was built in the 19th century, modeled after the Arch of Constantine. It originally stood at the entrance to Buckingham Palace, but it was moved during an expansion.

9   "Alice! Hi!"

Chise is here to meet Alice. Ruth is hiding in Chise's shadow, on guard in case Alice poses a threat.

10   "Well, that's why I wrote a letter."

See chapter 20.

11   "What alchemists usually do is reanimate animal corpses to serve as messengers."

Alchemists use their alchemy to control dead birds or animals and make them do their bidding. Unlike mage's familiars, this requires no "bond" between souls. Alice herself calls this one a "messenger bird" here, rather than a "familiar." (See volume 6, page 62.)

141

given on Christmas, and the custom of St. Nicholas' Day died out. The notion that Santa Claus brings presents on Christmas became widespread by the 19th century.

Japan has a practice of giving New Year's gifts, but this comes from the Chinese practice of offerings on the day celebrating the god of the heavens.

14 "Wow, look at those two eat...!" "They're really packing it away."

Living in England doesn't really give you a lot of opportunities to eat this kind of "typical English food for tourists." This would ordinarily be far too much food for two women, but given their magic and alchemy training, Chise and Alice seem able to handle it. Hopefully.

15 "I guess I don't mind going along."

Alice and Chise each have reasons for avoiding getting close to others. Neither of them have had the sort of warm family ties that lead to presents, so they have no experience with what sort of things make good gifts.

13 "So, um...this is about finding a Christmas gift..."

Alice wanted to talk to Chise about what to buy Renfred for Christmas.

The custom of giving Christmas presents springs from the ancient Roman Empire festival of Saturnalia, a celebration honoring Saturn, the god of the harvest. Later on (sometime around the 4th century), Saturnalia became a celebration of the Christian nativity, and the custom of gift-giving was redefined as commemorating the gifts brought by the Three Wise Men. The tradition spread along with Christianity.

Meanwhile, Santa Claus is modeled on the Christian St. Nicholas, from the Dutch name "Sinterklaas." December 6th is St. Nicholas' Day, and in keeping with legends about Nicholas saving children, children are given candy and presents. This custom originated in Holland in the 14th century and spread across Europe by the 16th.

In 1535, the German Martin Luther declared that such presents should be

You don't often see Chise with a gentle, bashful smile like this.

18 "Um?"

The centaur we saw earlier reappears, now on his way to deliver Elias' package to Angelica.

Angelica's shop in in London, near Westminster (see volume 1, page 58, where you can see the famous clock tower), which is within spitting distance of Hyde Park.

16 Magic Construct Following Chise. I

Chise nearly lost Alice in the crowd, but this construct is keeping a close eye on her.

17 "I'd say that makes us comrades."

This is the first time Chise's ever been close to someone roughly her own age who stands on equal footing with her.

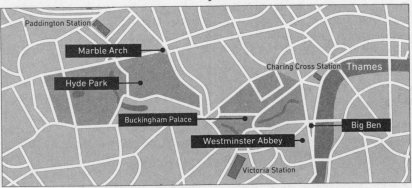

The landmarks that appear in chapter 26 are located as shown above.
The Marble Arch is to the northeast of Hyde Park.

21 "We centaurs also like such things as arrowheads or good, strong timber. Embroidery thread, dyes for fabric...that sort of thing."

Centaurs are famed for their skill with archery. They need good wood and arrowheads for that.

22 "Folks can be very particular when it comes to tools for their field of expertise."

Alchemist or a mage, each practitioner has their own style. If a gift doesn't fit that style, it'll be difficult for them to make use of.

23 "Hey! Alice, that you?"

Junkies from Alice's past.

Getting mixed up in drugs even once can lead to pushers coming after you, trying to get you to dip your hands back in. It's not a past that can be easily escaped.

19 "We're as hidden from their eyes as we are from ordinary folk."

Chise was born with the ability to see faeries, but alchemists are unable to see Hazel. Marking a cross with his hoof seems like a cantrip to make himself visible to Alice.

20 "Just tap an old stone on a hazel branch twelve times and I'll come running. I hear that little cantrip from anywhere!"

The centaur's name is Hazel, like the tree, and his name leads to a method of summoning him. Faeries like him, whose lives are connected to humans, often have some set means for humans to get in touch with them, which can range from chanting certain words where you first met them to weirder things like "Blow your nose loudly into a handkerchief at night."

From a different perspective, the means of calling neighbors is a form of summoning magic. Perhaps old tales of contracts formed between human and neighbor based on mutual good intent were handed down like magical rituals to summon them. The American spiritualist Judika Illes has a book of 5,000 spells, many of which involve summoning spirits and faeries—including spells that use hazelnuts as part of the summoning ritual.

Spiritualism has been popular in the west since the Middle Ages, and the process of drawing a magic circle on the floor, chanting a spell, and offering a sacrifice to summon a ghost or demon is quite well known. The words of the spell often invoke the protection of God or gods, so that even if the spirit or demon being summoned would harm the summoner, the fear of God will prevent them from doing so.

How to Summon Faeries

If humans are lucky enough to capture or aid a faerie or other neighbor, the faerie may promise to grant the human's wish in exchange for their freedom or to repay the debt. This may involve them telling the human how to call them, or saying that they can be found in a particular place at a particular time.

This is a form of contract between a human and a neighbor, and if the human breaks the promise, gets greedy, or tries to use the wish for evil, the contact is void and they'll never be able to summon the neighbor again.

In the Grimm fairytale "The Fisherman and His Wife," a fisherman catches a flounder and releases it, and is told that if he makes a wish while facing the sea, the wish will be granted. But when his greedy wife wishes to become a god, the couple loses all the wealth they've gained, along with the means of having wishes granted.

Dogs are often regarded as harbingers of death. In the 1998 movie *Black Dog*, there's a scene where a truck driver sees a vision of a Black Dog and gets in an accident.

Since the man in the black jacket drew a knife, Ruth doesn't hesitate to use his own harbinger powers. The man likely saw a vision of his own coming death.

Chise and Alice were walking through an alley near Soho. Soho has a history as an entertainment district, so it's an obvious spot to run into trouble.

24 Magic Construct Following Chise. II

The magic construct watches carefully as the junkies harass Alice and Chise.

25 WHUMP

Obviously a vulnerable spot on the average man. Alice is protecting Chise here, too, so she shows no mercy. In the panel above, Chise is whispering something to Ruth.

26 "I made sure they were in no shape to follow."

In a legend from the Isle of Man, in the 18th century, the spirit of a Black Dog haunted Peel Castle on the west coast of the island, frequently startling the guards. One soldier who scoffed at the stories and went out on patrol alone came running back screaming, and died three days later.

This Black Dog was called the Moddey Dhoo in the Manx language. There are legends from many places that those who see Black Dogs will soon die, so Black

29   28   27   26

International Day against Drug Abuse and Illicit Trafficking (June 26th) and used as part of a major anti-drug campaign that same year. "Zettai. Dame." ("Absolutely Never.") This public awareness campaign was a joint effort between the Ministry of Health, Labour and Welfare, the prefectures, charitable corporations, and the drug and stimulant abuse center. Until 2012, a number of celebrity campaign girls appeared on posters, but from 2013 to 2016, they used a mascot character called "Zettai. Dame-kun."

The mascot character "Zettai. Dame-kun," an anthropomorphized Earth, used since 2013.

27   "Did you, um…enjoy taking drugs…?"

Drugs sold on the street are often cut with other substances and are not very good.

England doesn't have a particularly high problem with drug addiction, but they do have a history of it, including the Opium War.

In the late 19th century, England was importing porcelain, silk, and tea from the Qing dynasty, and paid for it all by importing opium from the Indian colony into China. But when the Qing dynasty started clamping down on opium, military clashes broke out, leading to the Opium War.

England sent a fleet of sixteen ships, wresting control of the seas from the Qing. The war lasted two years, ending with England's victory.

28   "I was taught drugs are bad, end of story."

Chise is referencing a Japanese slogan from 1987 that was created for the

30

and Hinduism refer to this state as "Samadhi," considering it quite significant; much research was done on employing lengthy meditation or yoga practices to induce Samadhi.

However, in the mid-19th century, a means of isolating cocaine was discovered, and it quickly spread through England. At the time, the harmful side effects and addictive properties were not clear, and anyone could easily acquire it. In the magical world, it allowed easy entrance into trance states, and drugs became as widely used as alcohol and sex during magical rituals.

At the heart of this practice was a real modern magician, the infamous Aleister Crowley. He was born in England in 1875, and during a visit to Asia in 1900, he learned yoga arts, which he blended with Kabbalah and western magical traditions to develop his own methods, which he called magick. These made heavy use of drugs, and were known only to members of his A∴A∴ organization.

29 Magic Construct Following Chise. III

The magic construct watches Chise from the water.

30 The Alchemist and the Junkie

Alchemy, magic, and the drug trade have a long, close-knit history. When Native American shamans were communing with spirits, they used song, dance, and hallucinogens harvested from plants, and they prophesied or offered advice based on the resulting visions.

In India or medieval Europe, people made use of well-known poisons like nightshade or plants of the datura genus.

The reason people used these plants despite knowing the dangers is that the plants allowed them to enter an enhanced state of consciousness (or trance state) that could be essential when performing magic. In that state, practitioners feel at one with God or the universe, feel a wave of boundless joy, and feel as if they have become an all-powerful being. Buddhism

SUMMARY

Alice tells Chise how she met Renfred and became his bodyguard.

The medicine Renfred gave her allowed Alice to get through her drug withdrawal, but while training as his bodyguard, she makes a mistake that leaves Renfred scarred. Alice is guilt-ridden over allowing him to be injured, but that's the point at which their relationship begins to change.

Chise and Alice both acquire gifts for their masters and return home. Elias, who has been watching Chise via a magus craft, scolds her, but the unexpected gift surprises him. He thanks her. In return, he gives her a large teddy bear and says they'll open the other presents the next day.

Chise falls asleep, amazed to find herself genuinely looking forward to the morning.

CHAPTER 27　God's mill grinds slow but sure. II

General Remarks

The first half of this chapter shows how Alice and Renfred met and how she adjusted to her role as his bodyguard. Renfred is the first person in Alice's life who was willing to protect her even if it meant getting hurt himself—the first adult worthy of her trust. Alice's earnestness and Renfred's honest trust are a contrast to the messier relationship Chise and Elias share.

The latter half charms readers with the awkward gift exchange between Chise and Elias, and Chise is overwhelmed by new emotions when she learns how many other people sent her gifts.

Chapter Title

Continued from the previous chapter, the second part of "God's mill grinds slow but sure."

The original meaning of this phrase was that you must always pay for bad deeds, but that the payment is not always a bad thing. Good deeds may result in payments in kind.

Alice committed crimes while addicted to drugs, but in exchange for her suffering, she escaped withdrawal. Chise is scolded for slipping out without telling Elias, but the gift she got for him leads to happiness. Just as Renfred is rewarded for saving Alice, Elias gets a reward he never expected for the gift he made for Chise.

A continental breakfast is often found in hotels. There, the menu is generally composed of things served cold.

3 "The inside's different from the outside?"

Alchemists are cautious types who place magical protections on their homes so that the interior layout can't be determined from outside.

4 Mikhail Renfred

Renfred's full name is revealed. "Mikhail" is the Russian variant of the archangel Michael's name, and it's a common name

1 "An adequate amount."

The test tube placed on Alice's forehead contains manmade crystals—see volume 1, page 72, "a stone alchemists use for practice"—or something quite similar. They react to the magical energy Alice gives off by changing shape.

2 Title Page

Chapter 27's title page depicts an English breakfast. This is the traditional English breakfast (sometimes called a full breakfast): sausage, sautéed mushrooms, fried eggs, baked beans, tomatoes, toast, and fruit, served with coffee or tea. According to *Merkmal*, page 77, Renfred and Alice are both coffee people. Unlike the continental breakfast, the English prefer heaping piles of food, and according to the English writer W. Somerset Maugham, "To eat well in England you should have breakfast three times a day."

6   "It was probably medicine to make the withdrawal easier on me."

"Withdrawal" is the term for the symptoms that appear when one stops taking a particular drug. Depending on the drug in question, these can be anything from irritability or anxiety to shaky hands to hallucinations, and in some cases can even prove fatal—you can't just stop taking drugs without specialized medical care. It seems the magical medicine Renfred prepared didn't so much reduce the withdrawal as heal the damage the drugs did to her body. Of course, modern science isn't able to do that at this point.

for Russian men. Since Renfred is a common western name, his given name suggests he's half-Russian.

5   "Do you use drugs because you chose to, Alice?"

Drug addiction can manifest in two ways. Some people chase ever-greater highs, steadily increasing their quantity and frequency of use—positive reinforcement. Others use the drugs to escape the irritability and anxiety that occur after the drugs wear off—negative reinforcement. Both lead to higher tolerance levels as the addiction worsens, but here Renfred may be attempting to assess which situation Alice is in.

The author notes, "He's asking if she willingly put herself into this situation while aware of the risks. That will affect whether or not the medicine he makes to flush it out of her system will be painful for her." This sort of disciplinary approach involves positive reinforcement that will push her away from undesirable behavior.

10 "Just make sure you read every title and remember where you put them."

What matters to an alchemist isn't only the knowledge they hold in their head but the ability to quickly lay hands on a book that contains specific information they need. There's no way to memorize all the knowledge out there, so the first step is to have a solid grasp on where knowledge can be found.

11 "Getting him to read it for me would be a huge pain."

When facing irregular situations, it's best practice to report, communicate, and assess. The same applies to alchemist training. Alice quickly pays for this lapse in protocol.

12 The Monster from the Book

A book guardian with massive talons. It seems likely that it was designed to attack anyone who opened the book indiscriminately or anyone who opened it without

7 "Alice, opportunity has come knocking."

Abused by her parents and forced to deal drugs, Alice has never been given a choice until Renfred presents her with one. Given Renfred's attitude towards Elias and other non-humans, he has always seemed quite harsh, but here we see a gentler side.

8 "A bodyguard? Me?"

If it comes down to a fight, she'll be the alchemist's sword, and a shield that protects him.

9 "They stuck around just long enough to make me a junkie, too, before they both ODed and died."

Unfortunately, there are many cases of addicted parents giving drugs to their children. As awful as it may sound, they often give hungry children drugs to stop their crying.

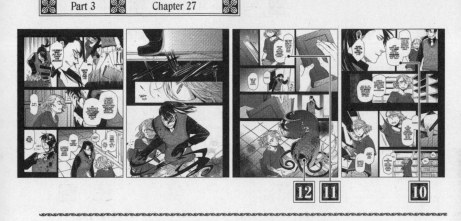

that anyone who stole or damaged the book would be punished by excommunication, damnation, or anathema. An anathema was the harshest of these, declaring that the subject and his entire clan would be sacrificed unto God. Some curses also went on to describe those who had fallen victim to these misfortunates, but most such examples were fabricated.

In the movie *Harry Potter and the Sorcerer's Stone*, Harry goes the library at night, searching for information about Nicholas Flamel. When he opens a restricted book, a face pops out and shocks him. This too is a type of book curse.

Not to get sidetracked, but that scene was filmed at Duke Humfrey's Library at Oxford, which, as in the movie, has a collection of valuable old books chained to the bookcases. Before the invention of the printing press, books were incredibly valuable, worth their weight in gold, and there were libraries throughout Europe that secured the books with chains so that they might not be stolen.

saying some sort of password. Traps like this are usually designed to prevent a book being stolen. Since this guardian returns to the book after lightly scarring Renfred, it may have been meant as more of a warning.

Spells designed to prevent books being stolen or copied without permission are known as book curses. The earliest known example is found on 7th-century BC tablets from the library belonging to Ashurbanipal, king of Assyria. "Whosoever shall carry off this tablet, or shall inscribe his name on it, side by side with mine own, may Ashur and Belit overthrow him in wrath and anger, and may they destroy his name and posterity in the land."

Historical and Fictional Book Curses

In medieval European churches and abbeys, it was common to find a book curse on the first page, written in the transcriber's hand. These curses often promised

under the influence of illegal drugs (the odds of withdrawal symptoms grow during long waits, making them harder to disguise), and the individual likely lacks the money for a private hospital, so they need to be able to deal with simple injuries themselves.

But according to the doctor, Alice's treatment techniques are just all kinds of wrong.

15 "Next time, I'll...I'll be a better bodyguard...! I won't let you get hurt again."

When Alice expresses her remorse, Renfred responds with trust. "I'll count on you next time," he says. This moment seems to be where they established the trust needed between an alchemist and a bodyguard.

16 "I guess I don't really know what to say."

Chise might understand how Alice did things, building trust through emotional conflict, but she can't identify with it, so she's not sure how to respond.

13 "You're finally healthy and whole. Don't be in such a rush for new scars."

Renfred is only concerned for Alice, not his own injuries. According to the self-psychology developed by Heinz Kohut, humans attempt to create an idealized version of themselves by raising a successor. By acting like their ideal mentor in front of children or students, they believe the child or student will grow up without the mentor's own flaws. To an alchemist, training a student is a crucial piece of their own training.

14 "I've got experience patching people up. I know how to do a good job...in my own way, at least. I've got no formal training."

The English National Health Service provides free health care at government-run hospitals, but it suffers from a shortage of staff and long wait times. Public health care poses a challenge for someone

18 Paddington Station

Paddington Station's distinctive arched design (known as the train shed) is the work of Isambard Kingdom Brunel and dates from 1854. Paddington Station features in mystery queen Agatha Christie's story "The Plymouth Express" and her novel *4.50 from Paddington*, so many bookworms will be familiar with the name.

19 "It's good you have a friend now."

The fact that Chise has a friend close to her own age makes Ruth happy enough that his tail is wagging. Quite a change in attitude from the previous chapter! (See volume 6, page 13.)

17 Walking and eating again

London has many food vendors selling sandwiches, burritos, or fish and chips. The word "sandwich" comes from the 18th-century English nobleman John Montagu, the Earl of Sandwich, who ate what we now call sandwiches while gambling. Yet Nicholas Rodger, the earl's biographer, states that the odds Montagu ever gambled are quite low, so the story may have been invented wholesale.

Similar foods were already an established presence in England by the 16th century, and were regularly referred to as "bread and meat" or "bread and cheese."

In the last panel of volume 6, page 61, we see another classic English dish: sautéed salmon. In England, it's common to take a later, more substantial midday meal and call it "dinner." After dinner, the evening meal might be called "tea" or "supper." Dinner can also occur in the evening, but if it does, lunch is a lighter affair.

23 "Am I 'upset' right now? Is that this feeling's name?"

Scolding a child who has done something wrong is similar to getting upset with them, but it's not quite the same. Elias hasn't lost his temper and started yelling at her. It's common to not realize just how angry you are when you're really mad, but Elias has had no means of identifying the emotions related to anger, so he needs the help of his teacher of human ways.

24 "Oh. Er... Yes."

He knew about the concept of giving Christmas presents, but wasn't expecting to receive one from Chise. It takes him a moment to realize that the present she's holding up is intended for him.

25 "U-Um... You always wear something kind of like that, so..."

Chise's present is a Bolo Tie (also known as a Bola Tie or a Bootlace Tie), a type of neckpiece made of a cord and a clasp.

20 "You were out quite late."

As Chise arrives home, so does the magical construct. Elias' expression never changes (it is made of immobile bone, after all), but that makes it all the more frightening for her.

21 "Were you watching the whole time...?!"

It never occurred to Chise she might be being watched, but peeping at someone using a familiar or magical construct can mean the difference between life and death, so to a mage the notion of respecting privacy holds little sway. As Elias has observed in the past, there are people everywhere after sleigh beggy.

22 "You're still wearing your stone amulet."

The stone amulet hanging from Chise's neck tells Elias where she is. See chapter 1.

28 **"Hmm? What's all that?"**

A present for Chise has arrived from Angelica. Chise wasn't expecting anything; like her master, she is unused to kindness from others.

29 **"Gifts for children should be placed beneath the tree."**

In the west, it's common to leave milk and cookies under the Christmas tree. When Santa Claus arrives, he drinks the milk and eats the cookies, and then leaves presents in return.

Invented in the 1940s, they became popular in the 1950s among a group of young men known as the Teddy Boys.

26 **"And here is your present."**

Elias' present (which we saw him sewing at the start of chapter 26) is a teddy bear. Stuffed bears are called "teddy bears" after the 26th American president, Theodore Roosevelt, who was nicknamed "Teddy." On one occasion when Roosevelt went bear hunting in 1902, his assistants caught and weakened a bear, hoping to allow the president to finish it off. In the name of sportsmanship, he refused. This inspired a cartoon in *The Washington Post*, which in turn inspired a line of stuffed bears.

27 **SNIFF SNIFF**

Either it has an unusual smell or it smells of Elias' "trick"; either way, Ruth is investigating the teddy bear's scent.

But what touched her most is the small happiness of having presents to open in the morning—a simple pleasure that everyone should have, but that has only now come back to her.

30 **"Alice and I had some girl-talk today, and that stuff's a secret."**

The fact that Alice talked about her past is now a precious memory for Chise.

31 **Snow on Christmas night**

Alice, Angelica, Molly (from Ulthar), Lindel, and the leannán sídhe—all the people with bonds to Chise—passing their own Christmases. Elias and Silky are lighting candles, presumably as part of a Yule custom hoping for the sun's return.

32 **"For the first time in a long, long time, I'm actually looking forward to tomorrow."**

With no religious significance to it, Christmas is often just another event to Japanese people, but Christmas and Yule are times of celebration designed to keep bad things at bay.

This is likely the first time Chise has celebrated Christmas in the full historical and mythological context.

from Scandinavia, but England already had a word that equates to Yule ("Jiuli"), so others think it was held even before the Norman Conquest.

The log used in the fireplace on Christmas Eve is called a Yule Log. The cake modeled after that is called a Buche de Noel.

Winter Solstice Festival

The winter solstice is the shortest day of the year, after which the length of time the sun is out increases, so many ancient religions had festivals celebrating the rebirth of the sun and marked that as the start of the year.

In northern Europe, before Christianity arrived, the winter solstice involved prayers for the return of the sun and plenty, as well as feasts to soothe the dead—the Yule festival.

During this Yule festival, they made offerings designed to restore the sun and to bring prosperity. In northern Europe, these offerings were made to Odin, god of war and magic.

Many things come out on the winter solstice. Everything from gods to witches,

DISCUSSION 5: Yule and Christmas

What is Yule?

Yule (aka Yuletide) is a winter solstice/New Year's festival celebrated by Germanic tribes in Europe, particularly the north, before the introduction of Christianity. Yule lasts for twelve days, from December 25th (modern-day Christmas) to January 6th (in modern times, the celebration of the Epiphany.) This is also called Twelfthtide, a cluster of several different holidays, but in the European tradition, holidays often start the night before, so things actually kick off on Christmas Eve. Some regions refer to it as the twelve holy nights—especially the eve of the Epiphany, which is called Twelfth Night and celebrated with feasts. Shakespeare's *Twelfth Night* was written to be performed on that twelfth day.

Yule was folded into Christianity and became a celebration of the birth of the messiah, Jesus Christ (Christmas = Christ + Mass). But in northern Europe, Christmas is still called Yule, and many elements of the festival (the Yule Log, Yule Goat, and Julebord) come from the original pagan festival.

Yule was celebrated everywhere from Scandinavia to Germany, and it was introduced to England early on. Some say the Norman invaders brought it with them

A Yule Goat, straw modeled after a sacrificial goat. They range from the size of your hand to the size of a two-story building.

The History of Christmas

What we now know as Christmas (the Mass of Christ) came into existence as Christianity spread across Europe, incorporating local pagan customs and turning them into a celebration of the messiah's birth. It started during the Roman Empire, mingling with Mithraism, and as it spread it added Germanic and Celtic traditions.

Currently in Christian traditions derived from the Catholic church (especially in England and America), the day Christ was born is given as December 25th (Christmas). January 6th is the day Christ was baptized in the Jordan River, the day

ghosts, and spirits are on the prowl, and packs of hunters and hounds led by gods or faeries (like the Wild Hunt) race across the sky, gathering the souls of the dead. The latter are sometimes called the Ride of the Souls, and described as the dead racing across the sky. Where they passed by, good crops were guaranteed. Some areas prepared a feast for these ghosts to calm them. This array of food was called the Julebord.

The Julebord refers to food prepared for a Christmas buffet.

As the winter solstice festival was intended to revive the sun, there were ritual sacrifices offered, and the goats sacrificed were called Yule Goats. These days, rather than kill a real goat, people decorate with goats made of straw and burn them during Yule or on the last day. Since Yule is also a time when the dead return, you see a number of similarities here to the Japanese obon festival.

thousand-year history of the Egyptian gods, especially the goddess Isis, vied for attention with the Zoroastrian sun god Mithra and with Christianity, with its new concept of monotheism and the practice of drinking wine during ceremonies.

Concerned about this state of affairs, the Emperor Elagabalus (reign: 218-222) attempted to fight these outside religions by promoting the worship of Sol Invictus, the unconquered sun god, setting the birthday on December 25th. Hippolytus, leader of one branch of the Roman church at the time, set Jesus' birthday on December 25th to compete.

Incidentally, the Egyptian goddess Isis also had her birthday set on December 25th, as did Mithra, a Zoroastrian god imported from Persia.

Even before that, the Romans had celebrated Saturnalia, a winter solstice and harvest festival dedicated to the god of agriculture, Saturn, from December 17th to December 25th. December 25th was dedicated to the solstice and the sun god, January 1st to the new year, and January 6th to Dionysus, god of fertility.

While the number of gods to worship grew in number, pretty much everyone was on board with having a big celebration at the end of the year. Later on, around 330, Emperor Constantine changed the sun god's name to Lux Mundi (light of the world), and he became the god of the Christian religion, since Christ had brought the light of justice to the world.

Arguments of whether Jesus's birthday should be celebrated at the time of his

his divinity was revealed—the Epiphany. But from a historical perspective, it's unclear when his birthday actually was (some theories even hold that he never existed).

Even among the early believers, there were a number of candidates suggested for the date of his birth, including March 28th, April 2nd, April 19th, November 8th, and November 18th. The idea that he was born in a manger and that shepherds in the fields quickly learned of his birth suggests it did not happen in winter, but Bethlehem is at the rather warm latitude of 31 degrees north, so there is some room for argument. Celebrations of the holy birth seem to have begun with the Gnostics, who argued over whether Christ's birthday or the Epiphany should be celebrated and settled on celebrating both at once.

Why December 25th?

The main reason December 25th was chosen was the existing religion in Roman times.

Originally, a lot of tribes (particular Germanic ones) celebrated the rebirth of the sun and the start of the new year at the winter solstice. This occurred roughly around what is now December 25th.

By the 3rd century AD, the Roman Empire no longer worshipped only their original gods (Jupiter and Neptune, etc.) but also a number of gods from Asia, Egypt, or the Celtic areas. In Rome, the

The practice of hanging ornaments from Christmas trees was already in place in Germany by the 16th century. People brought a fir tree indoors and decorated it with roses made from paper, or with apples, holy wafers, and rock candy. The practice spread among the upper classes, who threw parties designed to flaunt their wealth.

Santa Claus

The original form of Santa Claus was a god who arrived in winter, bringing the new year. He would threaten children and give presents to the good ones. This is very similar to the Namahage found in Japan.

Namahage is a festival tradition from the Oga Peninsula in Akita Prefecture. He's famous for asking if there are any bad children around.

birth/incarnation or the moment of his baptism were settled in 325 by the Council of Nicaea, which concluded that Christ was born the son of God and that December 25th was Jesus's birthday. That said, it took a few centuries for it to really settle in.

By making the existing winter solstice festival Christ's birthday, and by incorporating local sun god worship customs, Christianity was able to take root across all of Europe.

Origins of Christmas Trees

The custom of decorating a fir tree for Christmas comes from European tree worship.

At the start of winter, they would take young branches from firs, yews, and holly into their homes, trying to take the life-power of the evergreens for their own. This kind of custom is often seen in winter in areas with evergreens. In the past, it was often specific to a particular evergreen (like the fir), but records show that in the 18th century, at Nördlingen in Germany, they transferred cherry branches to pots, using the warmth of their homes to trick them into blooming in time for Christmas.

In Germany there is an old custom where children walk around town holding evergreen branches on December 28th. They tap people with the branches, ritually imbuing them with the branch's life force. Those tapped are believed to be granted good health.

This was brought into Christianity, and before Christmas, on December 6th, St. Nicholas and his terrifying servant Ruprecht would arrive and make sure children were saying their prayers properly. Children who hadn't prayed enough would be placed in Ruprecht's sack and carried away, but good children would be rewarded. These rewards would be handed out by a beautiful girl known as the Christkind (Christ child).

In this way, Germanic and Celtic traditions spread from Yule to Christianity. In the world of *The Ancient Magus' Bride*, these are traced back to their roots, and the Yule of ancient times is depicted.

CHAPTER **28** Look before you leap. I

SUMMARY

On Christmas morning, Chise is surprised to find flowers blooming on her new teddy bear's head. This is a trick Elias added, which absorbs Chise's magic and transmutes it into crystal flowers. Ruth says that they look tasty.

Chise goes out to thank Simon for his Christmas present, and Elias comes with her. They encounter a girl named Stella who's searching for her missing brother. Stella and her brother fought, and a neighbor with very old power, Ashen Eye, placed a spell on her brother and hid him.

In return for a promise of sweets, Chise and Elias make a pact to help Stella find her brother, and they begin looking, using the crystal flowers and Chise's blood as payment.

General Remarks

In the first half of the chapter, we find that the present Angelica sent Chise is a magic-suppressing bracelet to replace the ring that broke in chapter 22. While wearing it, Chise is almost unable to use magic at all.

In the latter half, without access to her magic, Chise barters her crystal flowers and her own blood, borrowing the neighbors' power to help Stella search for her brother.

Chapter Title

"Look before you leap" means to always prepare before taking action. Japan has a similar expression meaning "Use a cane before you fall."

The phrase comes from the words of 16th-century Englishman Richard Tottel and the 17th-century English poet Samuel Butler, and speaks of the importance of acting with caution and wisdom.

In this chapter, the saying refers to a careless turn of phrase on Stella's part, which allowed Ashen Eye to hide her brother. It could also be scolding Chise for acting emotionally and hurting herself.

And Caterpillar Fungus is...?

When Chise sees the flowers growing from her teddy bear, she compares them to a cutesy caterpillar fungus. She's thinking of a parasitic fungus that affects moth larvae and similar insects. The fungus is dormant in the winter, but when spring comes, it drains the larvae's nutrients and puts out stalk-like fungal filaments (killing the larvae in the process), with the "mushroom" fruiting body appearing aboveground in summer. That part generates spores, which infect new larvae.

The underground portion retains the shape of the larvae, leading to the species being described as "as insect in winter, grass in summer." The four kanji used to write that out form the Japanese name.

Technically, that name specifically refers to Ophiocordycepssinensis, which affects ghost moths, but in Japan the name tends to be applied to any fungus that's a parasite on insect larvae.

1 A Boy

The boy's name is Ethan. Ashen Eye finds him after he fights with his older sister, Stella.

2 Ashen Eye

A neighbor with ancient power who first appeared in chapter 20. Once it sets its sights on Ethan, the boy has no means of escaping.

3 Title Page

Chise dressed in full winter gear, interacting with some snowbugs. Possibly taking revenge for her treatment in chapter 19.

4 "Flowers...?!"

Chise is surprised to find flowers growing from the teddy bear's head. The flowers are made from crystal that changes form in response to magic, as seen in chapter 2.

Chise in chapter 23, it seems Chise's magic is almost entirely suppressed.

Perhaps they decided a ring wasn't large enough to handle Chise's power.

8 **"Most consider it stifling, but given how overtaxed your body is naturally, this ought to provide relief."**

Mages and alchemists absorb and produce magic unconsciously—it's as natural as breathing. We see this in action in volume 7, page 148.

9 **"I guess I can't send any messages, then."**

Letters are sent magically, in the form of birds, as seen in chapter 2. In chapter 26, Alice said it was "a shock when your paper bird came flitting up to me," so Chise has clearly learned this spell and was already making use of it in chapter 20.

5 **"They look tasty."**

Crystals that have absorbed magic from a sleigh beggy like Chise appeal to neighbors. This comment sets up events later in the chapter.

6 **"Dragons molt...?"**

Some creatures regularly shed their skin or scales as they grow—a process known as "molting." With some species, the process results in them leaving behind an empty husk or shell that holds their shape.

Among vertebrates, reptiles are especially known for shedding their skins. This shouldn't be taken to mean that dragons are related to reptiles, but in chapter 15 we learned that dragons can grow at will, so perhaps these sudden growth spurts require molting.

7 **The Bracelet Angelica Made**

To replace the ring that broke in chapter 22, Angelica made this bracelet. Once it's wrapped in the charm Shannon gave

he's accompanying her in order to keep an eye on her, since he doesn't trust her to do as she's told.

This foreshadows Elias' actions in chapter 30 and indicates that Elias' reasons for being "upset" with Chise in chapter 27 weren't as simple as they might have seemed.

13 "Have you seen a little boy around here?!"

This girl's name is Stella. She's the older sister of the boy we saw at the start of the chapter.

14 "What brother? She's our only child!"

Stella's parents are no longer aware that Ethan ever existed. When Chise realizes that, she immediately guesses that magic is at work, and asks Elias if she can get involved. This time, at least, she looked before she leaped.

10 "Everyone gave me such wonderful things, but I can't do anything for them in return."

It's only natural for adults to be generous to a young person Chise's age, but it doesn't feel normal to Chise. It makes her feel anxious, as if failing to repay other people's kindness will result in them abandoning her. It doesn't help that, without access to her magic, Chise feels as if she's lost her one strength.

11 "I'll start by doing whatever physical chores I can."

The things she's learned from Elias have given Chise confidence. According to Kohut's theory of self psychology, a person grows by amassing accomplishments, as we've seen Chise do. No magic can help a child grow.

12 "That was unusual..."

Since she's going to see Simon, and Elias isn't exactly Simon's biggest fan, Chise's surprised that Elias wants to join her. But

alone. But Elias has no obligation to get involved in crimes between humans.

17 "What payment will you offer?"

Elias borrows Chise's voice to demand compensation from Stella.

Magic is a powerful force, and if it's used for evil, the police aren't able to help. Its power means it shouldn't be used lightly, even to help others. Requiring payment puts limits on things, keeping the human borrowing the power and the mage using the power from drowning in it.

Simply paying money wouldn't be adequate compensation, as it would allow a human to borrow as much power as they can afford. What Stella offers—spending a set period of time working purely for the mage's benefit—is one good method of payment.

Things often demanded as payment by faeries include your next-born child, a glass of milk or cream left on the fireplace each day, or lending pots and pans to faeries who come asking, accompanied by a song. These are things related to the life

15 "When I couldn't find him, I ran back in and said Ethan was gone..."

As mentioned in the entry on changelings in chapter 23, faeries sometimes hide human children.

In Irish legends, faeries that live in marshes (or bogs) will kidnap children to play with, keeping them for a year and a day before returning them. Creatures like this are often called bogeymen in English-speaking countries, and are used to frighten children: "Go to sleep or the boogieman will get you."

In Japan, there are many regional legends of "kami-kakushi," in which gods or yokai will hide children (or even adults.)

16 "Had the child simply gone missing, it might have been an abduction."

Child abduction is a societal problem in England. According to figures provided by one charitable foundation, there are at least 70 kidnappings a day in London

18

four years later, following directions given in a dream. A fox disguised as an old man gave him a sword and a comb and said he should be raised to be king.

In the Edo period, when children were snatched away by Tengu, it was called "Tengu-sarai" or "Tengu-kakushi." The children would return in a few months or years, reporting that they'd been granted the wisdom of the Tengu, had flown with them to many places, or had been forced to pleasure men.

Kuñio Yanagita's *Tono Monogatari* collects a story called "Samuto no Baba," in which a young girl who lives in Samuto in Iwate Prefecture vanishes one day, leaving her zori lying beneath a pear tree. In the basis for this story, Kizen Sasaki's "Higashioku Ibun," it says the girl returned a few years later, wizened beyond her years like a yama-uba.

the human actually leads, and they have an immediate effect or restriction on the human's routine or livelihood.

18 **"Once a pact is made, it's proper for each party to show their true selves."**

Elias believes that since a pact involves an equal exchange, the parties involved must be on equal footing. He may be capable of changing his appearance, but showing Stella a false face would be unfair.

What is Kami-kakushi?

When a disappearance is blamed on "kami-kakushi" or "god hiding," it generally means that someone incurred the wrath of a god by entering the god's territory in the mountains or forest and breaking their rules.

According to *Azuma Kagami*, in the Heian period, Taira no Koremochi's third son encountered a kami-kakushi shortly after birth. He was found in a fox's den

21 **"I think it's a kind of ritual for finding things that are lost."**

The same "old technique for locating what's been lost" that Lindel used in chapter 16.

22 **"Someone is blocking it."**

Ashen Eye has lived far longer than Elias and is more powerful.

Magic and cantrips often fail, backfiring on the caster when they do. The best-known curse in Japan (the one that involves nailing a straw figure to a tree) will fail if someone sees it being performed, which kills whoever is trying to cast the curse.

The thread and spruce used here burn, but it's unclear if that's Ashen Eye's doing or if it's what always happens when the spell fails. Either way, Elias senses that he's at a disadvantage and doesn't make another attempt.

19 **"Nothing's as scary as the idea of my brother never coming home again!"**

In stories like Gabrielle-Suzanne de Villeneuve's *La Belle et la Bête*, children who meet unnatural creatures and aren't afraid often live happily ever after.

A folk legend from Donegal in Ireland tells of a brave boy named Jamie, who went to a faerie festival on his own, saved a girl the faeries had kidnapped, and married her. Connacht has a similar story about a boy named Guleesh.

20 **"Ohmigosh. It's so pretty! What is it?!"**

Chise's given her one of the crystal flowers from the teddy bear. Faced with an opponent that can hide children away, this might prevent Stella from being hidden herself. A second "look before you leap" moment.

25　　**24**　　**23**　**22**

Fables About Facing the Strange

In the Japanese folktale "Sen no Hari to Houtan," a giant snake grants a man a wish in return for the hand of his daughter in marriage. The man has three daughters, but only the youngest does not fear the snake. She demands a thousand needles and some gourds.

After sticking the gourds full of needles, she goes to the lake where the snake lives. She tells the snake that the gourds are important to her, and if he wants her as his bride, the gourds must all sink to the bottom of the lake. The snake agrees readily, but each time one gourd sinks, the others bob to the surface. As the snake struggles to sink them all, the needles in the gourds prick him and he cries out in pain. Eventually he gives up on the girl.

In the Grimm fairytale "The Frog Prince," we have a story of a princess forced to share a bed with a frog to get back a golden ball. When she reluctantly agrees, the curse is lifted and the frog becomes a prince, and the two live happily ever after.

23 **"Mind you, it's always highly probable that they'll try to deceive us to amuse themselves."**

Neighbors often take glee in tricking humans. Relying on their goodwill could result in being sent in the wrong direction.

However, if Chise pays equal compensation, as shown on later pages, both parties will be on equal ground and the neighbors have to tell the truth. Being honest and clever is vital when negotiating with faeries.

24 **"You have a problem?"**

A hawthorn spirit appears, drawn by Chise's magic.

25 **"Don't pay too much attention to any of this, okay? It's kinda dangerous for you."**

Stella has no way of negotiating with the fairies, so if she realizes they exist, it's possible that they'll pay attention to her and bring her misfortune. She's in enough trouble already.

Approximately 100cc—less than when giving blood.

29 "Of course I'm gonna worry! You're *hurt!*"

Stella's worried about her brother, but it's not in her nature to let Chise get hurt for her sake.

When dealing with faeries, it's important to have courage and remain unafraid, and to be forthright and sincere. These are your best weapons.

30 "We are not omnipotent."

Forcing an equal relationship with neighbors can sometimes be quite dangerous. It's also critical to remember that everyone has different strengths and weaknesses, and that some destinations can only be reached by taking what seems to be the long way around.

31 "Child of shadow, child of night... and a child of man, as well."

"Shadow" refers to Elias's nickname, Thorn (given the kanji "thorn of shadows").

"Night" is Chise, referring to the kanji given to "sleigh beggy."

26 The Centipede Faerie

Centipedes are arthropods of the Chilopoda class. The Japanese name is "mukade," and the kanji are "100" and "legs"—which, fascinatingly, is also what the English name means. As the names suggest, these creatures do have many legs, ranging from 15 pairs (30 legs) to 173 pairs (346 legs). They are carnivorous and will even bite humans, and are viewed as pests.

Japan has a legend about a large centipede yokai that lived on Mount Mikami, but after harming members of the dragon family, it was killed by Tawara Toda.

27 "Chise, set specific limits."

Elias determines that the centipede faerie has valuable information, so he allows Chise to take the risk of giving the faerie her blood. However, he prompts Chise to clearly specify how much the faerie can take from her (half a teacup full). If she weren't precise, she'd be running the risk of the faerie drinking her dry.

28 "Enough to half-fill a teacup."

In Japan, they prepare flower-decorated halls, in which lie Buddha statues representing the Buddha at the moment of his birth, and use ama-cha to represent the nectar. The Buddha's birthday is also known as "Hana-matsuri" or "The Flower Festival." After the introduction of the Gregorian calendar in the Meiji period, the date was set to April 8th, around when the cherry trees bloom, on the advice of Reigan Ando, a monk of the Jodo Shinshu.

There are many theories about when the Buddha was actually born. Theravada Buddhism, popular in Southeast Asia, celebrates Vesak (the birth, enlightenment, and death of the Buddha) on the 15th day of the second month of the Indian calendar.

In Islam, the birth of the prophet Muhammad is celebrated during Rabi' al-awwal (the third month of the Islamic calendar), somewhere between the 12th to the 17th, and is called "Mawlid." As the Islamic calendar has only 354 days in a year, this falls on a different day every year according to the western calendar.

Faerie manners dictate that one should rarely call another by their true name.

32 "Were you not the one who discarded this boy to begin with?"

The details become clear in the next chapter, but the gist is that during a sibling squabble, Stella told Ethan, "I didn't want a selfish, mouthy little brat for a brother, either!" That's what Ashen Eye is referring to. If Stella doesn't need Ethan, then Ashen Eye is free to take him.

What happens to children taken by faeries? Based on what we've seen with Shannon in chapter 23, we can safely say that it wouldn't be a happy ending for Stella.

Non-Christian Birth Festivals

In Japanese Buddhism, the Buddha's birthday is celebrated with memorial services on April 8th. These celebrations are rooted in the legends that say that when Siddhartha was born, the eight great dragon kings descended from heaven and made it rain nectar to bathe the newborn in.

SUMMARY

The search leads them to Ethan, but he remains in Ashen Eye's clutches. Ashen Eyes claims that Stella "discarded" Ethan, referring to what Stella said when she and Ethan were fighting.

Ashen Eye has severed the bond between Stella and Ethan, so the siblings can no longer even remember each other's names.

When Stella still wants her brother back, Ashen Eye proposes a game: Ethan and Elias are hidden elsewhere, and Chise and Stella have until sundown to find them.

Chise uses the fur Ashen Eye gave her to transform and locate Ethan and Elias. The siblings remember each other's names and return to find their parents' memories restored. Stella introduces Chise to her parents as a new friend.

General Remarks

This chapter shows the strength of Stella and Ethan's connection. Even after the fight, even after they blurted out that they didn't want each other, they miss each other and yearn for the family they've lost. Seeing the two of them makes Elias experience new emotions, and the search for Ethan turns Chise and Stella into friends, giving Chise a friend other than Alice—which also rattles Elias.

Chapter Title

Continuing from the previous chapter, we have the second part of "Look before you leap."

Even when arguing with family, there are some things you should simply never say. If a powerful neighbor overhears something spiteful, there's no telling what disaster could befall you. Stella and Ethan both spoke carelessly, leading to the bond between them being severed and then two of them being unable to recall each other's names.

"Look before you leap" means to think before you act, but in this case it also means to think before you speak. There's a reason we have so many expressions like "Loose lips sink ships."

why active children quickly get overheated and discard layers, but then when they get tired and slow down, they get cold just as fast.

4 Stella's Flashback

To a grownup, this might be a harmless squabble, but to children, each word carries far more weight than an adult might expect. They may hurt each other unintentionally sometimes, but by learning from those accidents, they learn how *not* to say hurtful things.

Neurological theory indicates that by hurting other people and feeling empathy toward their pain, we learn to mimic other's emotions in a type of brain cell called the mirror neuron.

1 Title Page

The happiest time in Chise's life contrasted with the present conflict between Stella and Ethan. Looking at the two of them, perhaps Chise sees the ideal sibling relationship she herself no longer has.

2 "We listen closely and hear clearly the words of humans."

Fae are called "neighbors" because they are always nearby. Japan also has the concept of "kotodama," in which words have the power to affect reality.

A similar philosophy is found in the Greek concept of "pneuma" and the Pacific Island concept of "mana." The world, or the air, is imbued with spiritual power that is influenced by words we speak. The power of words is one thing that makes spells and magic real.

3 "Zip up your coat!"

Children's bodies are small and don't retain heat as well as those of adults. They're much quicker to get hot or chilled. That's

is at work between two things that aren't directly connected.

In this case, the bonds of fate between Stella and Ethan have been severed, and the world itself altered so that the (direct) familial connection between them is fading away. Unless they can restore this bond, they'll become strangers to each other.

Ashen Eye has lived for thousands of years, so it's safe to assume it is well acquainted with the tenets of Buddhism.

8 "Although, perhaps I'll choose to relieve it of a limb or two—or add a limb or two instead."

As Shannon said in volume 5, page 89, humans taken to the Faerie Kingdom are unable to maintain human form. There's every chance Ethan would end up with a form as bizarre as Ashen Eye's.

9 "Don't!!"

Even faced with something as terrifying as Ashen Eye, Stella is driven forward by her feelings for her brother. Seeing her

5 Ethan

Ethan is unconscious and unable to resist. If he'd been able to speak here, perhaps things would have turned out differently.

6 "There's no telling what may hear those words...and take them to heart."

There are certainly neighbors that bear humans ill will, but far more frightening are those that take us at our word. If a powerful neighbor like Ashen Eye had heard Stella say, "I wish you were dead!" it could easily have thought, "Very well, I shall grant that wish," and made it come true.

7 "This is how it is when a bond is severed."

The word "en" (translated here as "bond") comes from Buddhism, and refers to indirect connections between things. Japanese people often say, "Kore monani ka no en" (literally "This, too, must be some sort of connection"), implying the hand of fate

12 "Now you two may search for them."

Ashen Eye proposes a challenge: before sunset, the girls must discover where Elias and Ethan have been hidden.

Faeries are known for presenting humans with challenges. In the Grimm fairytale "Rumpelstiltskin" (although the Germans pronounce it "Rumpelstilzchen"), the title creature offers a choice between giving up a child or guessing his name within three days.

The blue men of the Minch, said to appear along the Minch Strait in Scotland, are believed to shout two lines of poetry to passing ships. If those on the ship can't say the rest, the blue men will sink the ship.

Challenges offered by faeries are rarely fair, but if the human is unusually intelligent, they have a real chance of prevailing.

courage, Ashen Eye offers a proposal. Perhaps that was Ashen Eye's plan all along, but if Stella hadn't been so brave, it might well have changed its mind.

10 "You have nothing…"

Stella hasn't enough magic or other power to interest Ashen Eye. If she had the kind of artistic talent that attracts leannán sídhe, perhaps she could have traded that to Ashen Eye for her brother.

But at this point, Stella is just an ordinary little girl.

11 "You shall join us, child of shadow."

Ashen Eye dismisses a mage as powerful as Elias as easily as taking candy from a baby. In this moment we see just how powerful Ashen Eye really is.

This leaves Chise without Elias' advice, forced to play Ashen Eye's "game."

15 Ruth Talking Sense

They'd thought they'd found Ethan, only to have him snatched away, and the unfairness of it broke Stella's heart and left Chise frozen. It's up to Ruth to get them moving again.

Having a plan, even a simple one with low odds of success, is sometimes all it takes to motivate someone.

Practically speaking, they could use ropes to bracket off the terrain and search with human wave tactics, but whether Ashen Eye would allow that approach is an entirely different question.

16 "Use your animal nose."

Many four-legged animals have keener senses of smell than of sight. Many surface creatures can hide themselves well, so the heightened sense of smell makes it easier for predators to search for prey.

However, it seems Ashen Eye was wary of Ruth's nose, and has taken steps to disguise the smell.

13 "We're at too big a disadvantage."

When Chise points out that the challenge isn't fair, Ashen Eye makes a concession. For the contest to be balanced, Ashen Eye must have something at stake, but at the moment all it's offering is Ethan, who even Ashen Eye admits is merely an abandoned thing it claimed. So Ashen Eye offers a hint.

It seems Ashen Eye is aware that it's forcing this challenge upon them. Perhaps that's why it insists on calling this a "game" instead.

14 "Winter days are short."

England is at a high longitude, and the sun goes down especially early in winter. If we assume that it's currently around noon, Chise and Stella have only four hours until sundown.

19 "A-A monster!"

When Ethan wakes up and sees Elias, he instinctively responds the same way his sister did, prompting Elias to comment on the similarities between them. The fact that the siblings react the same way suggests they've seen the same movies, learned the same things from imitating their parents, and grown up in the same culture. It also demonstrates how close they really are.

20 "What's with your head? Is that real bone? Is it some kind of bone mask? Can you take it off? Or is that your real head?"

The intensity of a child's curiosity may be a little overwhelming for Elias. Elias isn't exactly the only one who'd react poorly to a question like, "Can you take it off?"

17 "'Animal nose'…?"

Ashen Eye's hint reminds Chise of the werewolf fur it gave her in chapter 20. Perhaps an animal with a stronger nose than a dog's could help.

When Chise became a fox in chapter 20, she almost forgot how to become human again. This could potentially be a scheme on Ashen Eye's part to make her transform again, moving her away from her humanity. But Chise insists it's safe, and says, "I've already decided where I belong."

18 "Where am I?!"

Ethan and Elias have been drawn beneath the water, which could be why Ruth said their scent was faint.

Elias may not need to breathe, but Ethan definitely appears able to do so, so Ashen Eye must have used some sort of spell or placed them close enough to the Faerie Kingdom that they're able to breathe underwater.

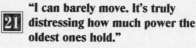

the other, or at least weaken Ashen Eye's power.

Possibly this is also Elias acting out of desperation (and lack of other options), but by making Ethan talk about Stella, he's trying to restore the severed bond.

23 "I'm eight years old! She doesn't have to act like I don't know anything!"

In England, primary education starts at the age of five. By the age of eight, children are socialized and beginning to understand how to act like upperclassmen to the younger students. Just as Stella tries to act like a good girl in front of her brother, her brother has started to insist that he deserves a certain level of respect, which is why Stella's lectures irritate him.

24 "Sharing a blood relationship with someone permits you to comprehend such emotional responses?"

Strong emotional connections between family members are called "human

21 "I can barely move. It's truly distressing how much power the oldest ones hold."

Elias' movements are restricted because they're inside a barrier Ashen Eye created.

By "barrier," we mean a space magically cut off by some means, preventing evil influence from entering, or trapping something inside.

In Japanese mountain faiths, a barrier is placed on sacred mountains to prevent the corruption of human civilization from encroaching on the mountains and to prevent the power sealed within the mountain from getting out.

Ethan seems to be able to move more freely than Elias, but he can't get past the barrier, either.

22 "If you two are thinking about each other simultaneously, it should make the search easier."

With the bonds of destiny between them severed, Elias thinks that perhaps the strength of their feelings can reach

To put it plainly, what Elias needs to understand the experience of human bonding is to raise a child himself. Raising another human, seeing the unconditional trust children have for their parents, and feeling the happiness generated by responding to that trust in kind—neurologically speaking, flooding you with oxytocin—is all necessary for understanding.

26 "Your family's the people who make you feel that way."

If being with someone makes you feel happy, that's the same as saying that bonding has occurred.

27 Elias' Eyes Widen

When Elias sees the fur come off and Chise transform back into herself, emotions well up within him. This is the moment when he understands what Ethan meant by, "I wanna see my mama and papa again. I wanna give them a big hug."

bonding" in psychology. Neurologically speaking, such connections are maintained by a balance of hormones like oxytocin, and blood or genetic connections are not (entirely) necessary. Bonding occurs between couples, with adopted children, and even with pets.

With siblings, assuming they were raised together, they've spent so much time together that the bonding conditions are met. Even without blood ties, they can predict even the smallest aspects of each other's behavior.

25 "I don't think I fully grasp the concepts of 'family' or 'husband and wife' yet."

Despite this lack of understanding, Elias has already referred to Chise as his "family" to Ethan. Elias is right that bonding can occur between members of "a unit that lives together for an extended period of time, each aiding the other's survival." That isn't the problem, here, though. It doesn't answer the question of why they were able to spend that much time together.

28

30 **"This looks far more delectable. You may have that bond back."**

Accepting the crystal flower Chise gave Stella as payment, Ashen Eye restores the bond between Stella and Ethan.

31 **"That was her intention!"**

The Japanese word used here ("kakushin-han") is used for crimes where the criminal believes their actions are justified, regardless of the law. But in recent years, it's begun to be used for crimes where someone knew what they were doing was wrong but did it anyway.

32 **"She toyed with us!"**

If Ashen Eye always intended to restore the bond in return for the crystal flower, then Chise and Stella's desperation was all in vain. But then, if they hadn't been desperate, Ashen Eye might have changed its mind.

Perhaps such speculation is unproductive.

28 **"Does that mean you don't want me to be your sister...?"**

Stella can't remember his name, but she's come looking for him just because he's her brother. The fact that she managed to find him gets through to Ethan.

The way his fingers touch her hand on his shoulder reveals his feelings for her.

29 **"What an amusing loss. Watching humans' earnest reactions is great fun indeed."**

Ancient beings have the power to twist human destiny easily. Just as Oberon changes the fates of four humans on a whim in *A Midsummer Night's Dream*, their presence nearby can be all it takes for awful things to happen.

But at the same time, neighbors have a powerful attraction to humans. As Ashen Eye says, "Human words hold power." Neighbors can't help being affected by that power, either. That's why Ashen Eye scolds Stella for speaking carelessly.

Battles of Wit with Faeries

Like the old Japanese story mentioned on page 171, there are many tales about intelligent, good young girls and boys defeating faeries and neighbors in battles of wit. This type of story generally shows that those who challenge faeries for good reasons, such as helping others, emerge victorious, while those who try to use the faeries' power for personal gain lose badly.

In the Finnish folktale "Jurma and the Sea God," the sea god threatens Jurma into giving the god three daughters. The older daughters break the sea god's rules, incur his wrath, and are thrown into a pit of tar. But the youngest daughter, Vieno, proves much smarter. She saves her sisters, deceives the tyrannical sea god, and makes off with a reward.

33 Their parents' memories are restored

Now that the bond is no longer severed, their parents remember Ethan, too. They've forgotten that they ever didn't.

34 "This is Chise! We just met! She's my new friend!"

Never the timid sort, Stella immediately introduces Chise as a friend. Chise looks less embarrassed than caught completely off guard. Part of her still finds it hard to admit that she's worth being friends with.

Since her relationship with Stella continues beyond chapter 30, their new connection leads to other actions on Elias' part.

conversations held with some sort of magical assistance.

So what language are the neighbors using? How do they acquire language?

Based on the story of Ruth's origins, it seems neighbors are born with an innate understanding of this language. It's hard to imagine anyone teaching Elias or the Will o' the Wisp how to speak. We can see many depictions of supernatural beings understanding language without anyone teaching it to them throughout myths and legends around the world. To cite a famous example, see the Old Testament Book of Genesis, where Adam understands the word of God from the very beginning (Genesis 1:28, 2:16, etc.).

The language God employed when speaking to Adam is known as "Adamic Language." The 16th-century alchemist John Dee referred to this as the "Language of Angels" or the "Holy Language." John Dee's writings also use a language called Enochian, from the language spoken by the patriarch, Enoch.

Ruth appears to understand language (presumably English) from the beginning, which is consistent with the idea of language as a divine gift. Now that he's shared knowledge with Chise, perhaps he can speak Japanese, too.

However, if this is true, it brings us to a more fundamental question: if language is something ingrained in the world's systems, then who made the languages we speak?

DISCUSSION 6: Words Linking Faerie and Human: An Evolutionary Linguistics Approach

Quite a variety of neighbors appear within this series, and all of them are depicted as being able to converse normally with Chise. (For example, volume 1, page 132, "Th-The cat just spoke?!")

We thought we'd examine the language of the faeries from both scientific and mythological standpoints.

Adamic Language

The round frames in which manga character dialogue appears are called "balloons." In this series, the dialogue of faeries, neighbors, and dragons is visually distinguished from that of humans via balloons drawn with a double line. Meanwhile, creatures with inhuman forms like Elias and the centaur (see volume 6, page 6) use standard balloons.

It's a common manga technique to use special balloons like these for dialogue heard over a phone or through some other broadcast method, but they're also used for foreign languages or alternative means of communication. Naturally, faeries aren't using telephones. Given that creatures whose vocal cords are different than those of humans (like Ulthar's cats and Black Dogs like Ruth) are depicted conversing this way, we can assume these doubled balloons indicate

An Approach Taken From Evolutionary Biology

Our brains had already evolved to their current size 300,000 years ago. If the size of the brain is tied to our capacity for intelligence, then our intelligence hasn't changed dramatically since then. But in fact many forms of knowledge, including language, seem to have been acquired only 150,000 years ago by even the most generous estimates, and there was an intellectual surge some 60,000 years ago, named the "Great Leap Forward" by Jared Diamond, author of *Guns, Germs, and Steel*.

According to an interpretation agreed upon by many academics, at some point during a range of time spanning tens or hundreds of thousands of years, our intellects suddenly began to develop—and yet our brains had attained the shape appropriate for handling that knowledge far earlier.

That means that even in the world of *The Ancient Magus' Bride*, humans and neighbors only began having cultural exchanges around that time. Did humans develop language and the neighbors imitate that, or did the neighbors have language first—a universal language like Adamic—which they transferred to us? Either seems possible.

But perhaps language is not the only thing exchanged between humans and neighbors.

The neuroscientist Vilayanur S. Ramachandran gave his students two images, one with rounded curves and one jagged (both arbitrary sketches containing no inherent meaning), and asked them, "Which is 'bouba' and which

Forbidden Research on Origins of Language

In 1859, *On the Origin of Species* was published. Until Darwin's theory of evolution became widely accepted, the notion that language was a gift from God had a lot of weight.

Something that has been frequently mentioned in comparative linguistic research is the 1865 Linguistic Society of Paris, which explicitly banned all discussion of the origin of language and the construction of the universal language. This latter concept was (according to the notions of the day) tantamount to discovering the true names of all things as given to them by Adam.

Even at the time, there were many academics arguing against the concept of language as a gift from God, but when it came to research on the origin of language or the universal language, it was impossible to avoid religious clashes in academic circles. The only means academics had to avoid the interference of religion was to argue for banning the subject outright. This speaks to how great a threat research on the origins of language was to Christian values.

Today the concept of language as a gift from God is widely rejected.

But within the world of *The Ancient Magus' Bride*, we do see a similar phenomenon. Where does that leave us? Perhaps merely shouting into the wind, but as a thought experiment, let's examine how languages come to be within the world of this series.

understand language as long as there is an intellect. Once the mind develops, language should be acquired in time, and if language is acquired, it should be possible to understand each other's languages. In evolutionary biology, this is known as convergent evolution.

But modern neurology tells us that all of our emotions spring from the workings of our nerve cells. When Chise cries because the leannán sídhe has lost Joel (volume 5, page 62), it's because her nerve cells are firing, and because her brain has that capacity. And when Elias looks at Chise and thinks, "Something inside me is...squirming" (volume 5, page 63), it's because that functionality exists inside that bone head of his. Convergent evolution of the intellect alone is not enough to explain why sympathetic connections are made between emotions.

Naturally, it's hard to believe that faeries have genes and procreate the way humans do, but from an evolutionary linguistics point of view (which searches for the origins of language via the evolutionary process), peering across to the other side, we can only conclude that faeries and humans split off somewhere between tens of thousands of years ago and the present day.

It isn't such a bizarre proposition to assume that while humans were acquiring language and other cultural progress during their "great leap forward," they had significant interaction with the neighbors—so much so that, at the time, it's unlikely that they had words to distinguish between neighbors and humans.

And isn't that an exciting concept in and of itself?

is 'kiki'?" In their answers, 98% of the students claimed the rounded one was "bouba" and the jagged one "kiki."

This trend was seen regardless of the respondent's native language, and was named the Bouba/Kiki Effect. In other words, whatever languages we speak, we share certain universal concepts mapping sounds to objects. It would be a leap from this to conclude that Adamic languages actually existed, but it does provide a clue as to how humans and neighbors are able to communicate.

The Bouba/Kiki Effect occurs because our brains are all made the same way, without magical differences between different races or genders. Further evidence for this is that this effect is not present in those who have damage to the angular gyrus, which controls visual language processing. It's another logical leap, but if neighbors understand language as we do and share common concepts, then neighbors' brains are almost identical to ours.

Sympathetic Connections

That said, the tiny skull of an ariel can't house a brain the same size as ours. We must assume that either some magic is at work here, or an effect of the world's systems as they exist within the series' framework. But be that as it may, evolutionary biology leads us to the conclusion that if there are this many traits shared between humans and neighbors, we most likely share a common ancestor.

Even without a common ancestor, you might think that it's only natural to

BOOKS

A Dictionary of Plant Lore, Roy Vickery. Japanese translation by Hiroaki Okamoto, published by Yasaka Shobo.

Dictionary of Symbols and Imagery, Ad de Vries. Japanese edition edited by Shuichiro Yamashita, published by Taishukan Shoten.

The Merchant of Venice, Complete Shakespeare 10, Shakespeare, Japanese translation by Kazuko Matsuoka, published by Chikuma Shobo.

Dictionary of English Proverbs, Takanobu Otsuka, Seizou Takase, published by Sanseido.

A Dictionary of Superstitions, Iona Opie and Moira Tatem. Japanese translation by Kazumi Yamagata, Masazumi Araki, Akinobu Okuma, Motoko Nakada, published by Tashukan Shoten.

The Roman Era: The British Isles: 55 BC-AD 410 (Short Oxford History of the British Isles), Peter Salway. Japanese Editor: Hirokazu Tsurushima. Supervising Translator: Takashi Minamigawa. Published by Taishikan Shoten.

Tales from a Finnish Tupa, J.C. Bowman and M. Bianco. Translation by Teiji Seta. Published by Iwanami Shoten.

Kayano Shigeru no Ainugo Jiten Souhoban, Shigeru Kayano, Publisher: Sanseido.

Kanyaku Grimm Douwa, the Brothers Grimm. Translation: Keigo Seki, Toyohiko Kawabata. Publisher: KADOKAWA/Kadokawa Shoten.

The Vampire Encyclopedia, Matthew Bunson, translated by Kazuya Matsuda, Publisher: Seidosha.

Black Athena: The Afroasiatic Roots of Classical Civilization (Volume 2: The Archaeological and Documentary Evidence), Martin Bernal. Translated by Kazuko Kanai. Publisher: Fujiwara Shoten.

Encyclopedia Celtica, Bernhard Maier, edited by Mayumi Tsuruoka, translated by Naoichiro Hiroshima, published by Sogensha.

Celt-jin no Rekishi to Bunka, Masatoshi Kimura. Publisher: Hara Shobo.

Celt Shinwa—Megami to Eiyuu to Yousei to, Kimie Imura, published by Chikuma Shobo

Dictionary of Celtic Myth and Legend, Miranda J. Green, supervising translator: Kimie Imura, translators: Junko Watanabe, Atsuko Ohashi, Kana Kitagawa, published by Tokyo Shoseki

Celt to Nihon, Toji Kamata and Mayumi Tsuruoka. Publisher: KADOKAWA/Kadokawa Shoten.

The Celtic Wisdom of Trees, Jane Gifford. Supervising translator: Kimie Imura, Translation: Masato Kurashima. Publisher: Tokyo Shoseki

Celt no Suimyaku, Kiyoshi Hara. Publisher: Kodansha.

Celtic Fairy Tales, Joseph Jacobs. Translation: Umeko Kotsuji. Publisher: Interplay.

Irish Fairy and Folktales, W. B. Yeats. Translation: Kimie Imura. Publisher: Chikuma Shobo.

The Historical Atlas of the Celtic World, John Haywood. Supervising Translator: Kimie Imura. Translation: Masato Kurashima. Publisher: Tokyo Shoseki.

A Dictionary of Modern English Proverbs. Editor: Yutaka Toda. Publisher: Liber Press.

Celtic Tree, Rieko Sugihara, published by Jitsugyo no Nihon Sha

Shigusa no Minzokugaku, Toru Tsunemitsu. Publisher: KADOKAWA/Kadokawa Gakugei Shuppan.

"Jikoai" to "Izon" no Seisin Bunseki: Kohut Sjinrigaku Nyumon, Hideki Wada. Publisher: PSP Kenyusho.

Constructing Evolutionary Linguistics. Editors: Koda Fujita and Kazuo Okanoya. Publisher: Hitsuji Shobo.

Zukai Celt Shinwa, Ryota Ikegami. Publisher: Shinkigensha.

The Illustrated Exploring the World of the Celts, Simon James. Supervisor: Kimie Imura. Translation: Akiko Yoshioka, Mitsuko Watanabe. Publisher: Tokyo Shoseki.

The Illustrated Exploring the World of the Druids, Miranda J. Green. Supervisor: Kimie Imura. Translator: Ken Oide. Publisher: Tokyo Shoseki.

Zusetsu Europe Saijiki: Doitsu no Nenchu Kouji, Masazumi Fukushima and Kazuhiko Fukui. Publisher: Yasaka Shobo

The Element Encyclopedia of 1000 Spells, JudikaIlles. Publisher: Setsuwasha.

Sekai Shinwa Jiten: Sousei Shinwa to Eiyuu Densetsu. Edited by: Taryo Oobayashi, Seiji Itoh, Atsuhiko Yoshida and Kazuo Matsumura. Publisher: KADOKAWA/Kadokawa Shoten.

Giants, Monsters and Dragons: An Encyclopedia of Folklore, Legend, and Myth, by Carol Rose, supervising translator Kazuo Matsumura, published by Hara Shobo.

Spirits, Fairies, Leprechauns, and Goblins: An Encyclopedia, by Carol Rose, supervising translator Kazuo Matsumura, published by Hara Shobo.

Higashioku Ibun, Kizen Sasaki. Publisher: Aozora Bunko.

Nihon no Minwa (Touhoku/Hokkaido-hen), Morihiko Fujisawa. Publisher: Gutenberg 21.

The Tell-Tale Brain: A Neuroscientist's Quest for What Makes Us Human, by V. S. Ramachandran. Translation: Atsuko Yamashita. Publisher: KADOKAWA/Kadokawa Shoten.

The Lilac Fairy Book, Andrew Lang. Supervisor: Junko Nishimura. Publisher: Tokyo Sougensha.

Frau Faust, Kore Yamazaki. Publisher: Kodansha.

The Ancient Magus' Bride Official Guide Book Merkmal. Editorial Supervisor: Kore Yamazaki. Editing: Mag Garden. Publisher: Mag Garden.

Moeru! Celt Shinwa no Megami Jiten, by TEAS Jimusho, published by Hobby Japan.

Encyclopedia of Fairyology, Kimie Imura, published by Tokyo Shoseki.

An Encyclopedia of Fairies: Hobgoblins, Brownies, Bogies, and Other Supernatural Creatures, by Katharine Briggs, translated cooperatively by Keiichi Hirano, Kimie Imura, Tadaaki Miyake, and Shin'ichi Kishida, published by Fuzambo.

Yousei no Sodatekata, Ryo Katsuragi. Publisher: Hakusensha

Medieval Holidays and Festivals, Madeline P. Cosman. Translation: Kyoko Kato, Toshiko Yamada. Publisher: Harashobo.

The Doomspell, Cliff McNish. Translation: Mizuhito Kanehara. Publisher: Rironsha.

WEBSITES
Iceland Abroad: Japan
Film Critic Tomohiro Machiyama's American Diary
Project Gutenberg
Internet Sacred Text Archive

A number of additional books and websites.

The
Ancient Magus'
Bride
Supplement
II